Don't Be Swindle

33 1/3 Global

33 1/3 Global, a series related to but independent from **33 1/3**, takes the format of the original series of short, music-based books and brings the focus to music throughout the world. With initial volumes focusing on Japanese and Brazilian music, the series will also include volumes on the popular music of Australia/Oceania, Europe, Africa, the Middle East and more.

33 1/3 Japan

Series Editor: Noriko Manabe

Spanning a range of artists and genres – from the 1970s rock of Happy End to technopop band Yellow Magic Orchestra, the Shibuya-kei of Cornelius, classic anime series *Cowboy Bebop*, J-Pop/EDM hybrid Perfume and vocaloid star Hatsune Miku – 33 1/3 Japan is a series devoted to in-depth examination of Japanese popular music of the twentieth and twenty-first centuries.

Published Titles:

Supercell's *Supercell* by Keisuke Yamada

AKB48 by Patrick W. Galbraith and Jason G. Karlin

Yoko Kanno's *Cowboy Bebop Soundtrack* by Rose Bridges

Perfume's *Game* by Patrick St. Michel

Cornelius's *Fantasma* by Martin Roberts

Joe Hisaishi's *My Neighbor Totoro: Soundtrack* by Kunio Hara

Shonen Knife's *Happy Hour* by Brooke McCorkle

Nenes' *Koza Dabasa* by Henry Johnson

Yuming's *The 14th Moon* by Lasse Lehtonen

Kohaku utagassen: The Red and White Song Contest by Shelley Brunt

Toshiko Akiyoshi-Lew Tabackin Big Band's *Kogun* by E. Taylor Atkins

S.O.B.'s *Don't Be Swindle* by Mahon Murphy and Ran Zwigenberg

Forthcoming Titles:

Yellow Magic Orchestra's *Yellow Magic Orchestra* by Toshiyuki Ohwada

33 1/3 Brazil

Series Editor: Jason Stanyek

Covering the genres of samba, tropicália, rock, hip hop, forró, bossa nova, heavy metal and funk, among others, 33 1/3 Brazil is a series devoted to in-depth examination of the most important Brazilian albums of the twentieth and twenty-first centuries.

Published Titles:

Caetano Veloso's *A Foreign Sound* by Barbara Browning

Tim Maia's *Tim Maia Racional Vols. 1 & 2* by Allen Thayer

João Gilberto and Stan Getz's *Getz/Gilberto* by Brian McCann

Gilberto Gil's *Refazenda* by Marc A. Hertzman

Dona Ivone Lara's *Sorriso Negro* by Mila Burns

Milton Nascimento and Lô Borges's *The Corner Club* by Jonathon Grasse

Racionais MCs' *Sobrevivendo no Inferno* by Derek Pardue

Naná Vasconcelos's *Saudades* by Daniel B. Sharp

Chico Buarque's First *Chico Buarque* by Charles A. Perrone

Forthcoming titles:

Jorge Ben Jor's *África Brasil* by Frederick J. Moehn

33 1/3 Europe

Series Editor: Fabian Holt

Spanning a range of artists and genres, 33 1/3 Europe offers engaging accounts of popular and culturally significant albums of Continental Europe and the North Atlantic from the twentieth and twenty-first centuries.

Published Titles:

Darkthrone's *A Blaze in the Northern Sky* by Ross Hagen

Ivo Papazov's *Balkanology* by Carol Silverman

Heiner Müller and Heiner Goebbels's *Wolokolamsker Chaussee* by Philip V. Bohlman

Modeselektor's *Happy Birthday!* by Sean Nye

Mercyful Fate's *Don't Break the Oath* by Henrik Marstal
Bea Playa's *I'll Be Your Plaything* by Anna Szemere and András Rónai
Various Artists' *DJs do Guetto* by Richard Elliott
Czesław Niemen's *Niemen Enigmatic* by Ewa Mazierska and Mariusz Gradowski
Massada's *Astaganaga* by Lutgard Mutsaers
Los Rodriguez's *Sin Documentos* by Fernán del Val and Héctor Fouce
Édith Piaf's *Récital 1961* by David Looseley
Nuovo Canzoniere Italiano's *Bella Ciao* by Jacopo Tomatis
Iannis Xenakis's *Persepolis* by Aram Yardumian
Vopli Vidopliassova's *Tantsi* by Maria Sonevytsky
Amália Rodrigues's *Amália at the Olympia* by Lila Ellen Gray
Ardit Gjebrea's *Projekt Jon* by Nicholas Tochka
Aqua's *Aquarium* by C.C. McKee
J.M.K.E.'s *To the Cold Land* by Brigitta Davidjants
Taco Hemingway's *Jarmark* by Kamila Rymajdo

Forthcoming Titles:
Tripes' *Kefali Gemato Hrisafi* by Dafni Tragaki
Silly's *Februar* by Michael Rauhut
CCCP's *Fedeli Alla Linea's 1964–1985 Affinità-Divergenze Fra Il Compagno Togliatti E Noi Del Conseguimento Della Maggiore Età* by Giacomo Bottà

33 1/3 Oceania

Series Editors: Jon Stratton (senior editor) and Jon Dale (specializing in books on albums from Aotearoa/New Zealand)
Spanning a range of artists and genres from Australian Indigenous artists to Maori and Pasifika artists, from Aotearoa/New Zealand noise music to Australian rock, and including music from Papua and other Pacific islands, 33 1/3 Oceania offers exciting accounts of albums that illustrate the wide range of music made in the Oceania region.

Published Titles:

John Farnham's *Whispering Jack* by Graeme Turner

The Church's *Starfish* by Chris Gibson

Regurgitator's *Unit* by Lachlan Goold and Lauren Istvandity

Kylie Minogue's *Kylie* by Adrian Renzo and Liz Giuffre

Alastair Riddell's *Space Waltz* by Ian Chapman

Hunters & Collectors's *Human Frailty* by Jon Stratton

The Front Lawn's *Songs from the Front Lawn* by Matthew Bannister

Bic Runga's *Drive* by Henry Johnson

The Dead C's *Clyma est mort* by Darren Jorgensen

Ed Kuepper's *Honey Steel's Gold* by John Encarnacao

Chain's *Toward the Blues* by Peter Beilharz

Hilltop Hoods' *The Calling* by Dianne Rodger

Screamfeeder's *Kitten Licks* by Ben Green and Ian Rogers

The Triffids' *Born Sandy Devotional* by Christina Ballico

5MMM's *Compilation Album of Adelaide Bands 1980* by Collette Snowden

The Clean's *Boodle Boodle Boodle* by Geoff Stahl

The Avalanches' *Since I Left You* by Charles Fairchild

Soundtrack from *Saturday Night Fever* by Clinton Walker

John Sangster's *Lord of the Rings, Vols. 1-3* by Bruce Johnson

Forthcoming Titles:

INXS' *Kick* by Ryan Daniel and Lauren Moxey

Sunnyboys' *Sunnyboys* by Stephen Bruel

Eyeliner's *BUY NOW* by Michael Brown

silverchair's *Frogstomp* by Jay Daniel Thompson

TISM's *Machiavelli and the Four Seasons* by Tyler Jenke

The La De Das' *The Happy Prince* by John Tebbutt

Gary Shearston's *Dingo* by Peter Mills

Crowded House's *Together Alone* by Barnaby Smith

Don't Be Swindle

Mahon Murphy and Ran Zwigenberg

Series Editor: Noriko Manabe

BLOOMSBURY ACADEMIC
NEW YORK • LONDON • OXFORD • NEW DELHI • SYDNEY

BLOOMSBURY ACADEMIC
Bloomsbury Publishing Plc
1385 Broadway, New York, NY 10018, USA
50 Bedford Square, London, WC1B 3DP, UK
29 Earlsfort Terrace, Dublin 2, Ireland

BLOOMSBURY, BLOOMSBURY ACADEMIC and the
Diana logo are trademarks of Bloomsbury Publishing Plc

First published in the United States of America 2025

Copyright © Mahon Murphy and Ran Zwigenberg, 2025

For legal purposes the Acknowledgements on pp. xi–xii constitute
an extension of this copyright page.

All rights reserved. No part of this publication may be reproduced or
transmitted in any form or by any means, electronic or mechanical, including
photocopying, recording, or any information storage or retrieval system,
without prior permission in writing from the publishers.

Bloomsbury Publishing Inc does not have any control over, or responsibility
for, any third-party websites referred to or in this book. All internet addresses
given in this book were correct at the time of going to press. The author and
publisher regret any inconvenience caused if addresses have changed or sites
have ceased to exist, but can accept no responsibility for any such changes.

Whilst every effort has been made to locate copyright holders the publishers
would be grateful to hear from any person(s) not here acknowledged.

Library of Congress Cataloging-in-Publication Data
Names: Murphy, Mahon, author. | Zwigenberg, Ran, 1976- author.
Title: Don't be Swindle / Mahon Murphy and Ran Zwigenberg.
Other titles: S.O.B's Don't be Swindle
Description: [1.] | New York : Bloomsbury Academic, 2025. |
Series: 33 1/3 Japan | Includes bibliographical references.
Identifiers: LCCN 2024029345 (print) | LCCN 2024029346 (ebook) |
ISBN 9798765108963 (paperback) | ISBN 9798765108956 (hardback) |
ISBN 9798765108987 (pdf) | ISBN 9798765108970 (ebook)
Subjects: LCSH: S.O.B. (Musical group : Japan). Don't be Swindle. |
Punk rock music–Japan–Kyoto–History and criticism. |
Grindcore (Music)–Japan–Kyoto–History and criticism. |
Rock music–Japan–1981–1990–History and criticism.
Classification: LCC ML421.S17 M87 2025 (print) | LCC ML421.S17 (ebook) |
DDC 781.660952/1864–dc23/eng/20240709
LC record available at https://lccn.loc.gov/2024029345
LC ebook record available at https://lccn.loc.gov/2024029346

ISBN:	HB:	979-8-7651-0895-6
	PB:	979-8-7651-0896-3
	ePDF:	979-8-7651-0898-7
	eBook:	979-8-7651-0897-0

Series: 33 1/3 Japan

Typeset by Integra Software Services Pvt. Ltd.
Printed and bound in Great Britain

To find out more about our authors and books visit
www.bloomsbury.com and sign up for our newsletters.

Contents

List of figures x
Acknowledgements xi

Introduction 1

1 **I'm a dreamer: The origins and infrastructure of the Kyoto scene (1968–80)** 17

2 **Speed my way: The organization of the wider Kyoto punk scene, 1977–86** 33

3 **Look like devil: Who are the punks?** 45

4 ***Don't Be Swindle*** 57

5 **Heads or tails? The live scene after *Don't Be Swindle*** 69

6 **To be continued? Kansai hardcore goes global** 83

Conclusion 95

Bibliography 102
Index 112

Figures

1A and 1B   S.O.B. posing on the back cover of Don't Be Swindle (courtesy of S.O.B.) 3

2   Seibu kōdō has seen better days but the three stars remain prominently displayed on the roof 20

3   Seki's (centre) pre-S.O.B. band the Bones performing at a 1985 Beat Crazy Event inside Seibu kōdō (photo courtesy of Minamitsuji 'Babi' Akihiro) 39

4   Imai's alternative design for *Don't Be Swindle*'s cover art was included as a sticker with the album and in poster art for the band's European tour (courtesy of S.O.B.) 51

5   Detail from the back cover showing the track listing and Naoto's apocalyptic artwork (courtesy of S.O.B.) 58

6   A different impression of Seibu kōdō, as it hosts debates during the X-Day event (courtesy of Kyoto University Newspaper Photo Archives 京都大学新聞写真アーカイブ) 76

7   Young female S.O.B. fans gather outside Seibu kōdō in June 1990 (copyright, Ota Junichi) 85

8   Imai, Seki and Yasue still representing Kyoto's Punk Scene in 2021 96

Acknowledgements

There are many people to thank for making this book possible. First, we should thank the current members of S.O.B., Yasue, Seki and Imai for helping us put together this story and patiently answering the myriad of questions we had. Just as S.O.B. would get nowhere without their roadie, Kanda, nor would we have progressed without his knowledge of the punk scene in Kyoto and donation of valuable research material. We would like to thank all the interviewees for being so generous with their time: Oguma Eiji, Ito Kimio, Babi, Ishibashi Shōjirō, Makita Naoko, Mōri Yoshitoka, Ōhara Mitsuo, Ta-Ko, Ugaya Hiromu and Wada Ryoichi. The Kyoto punk scene also provided venues for us to conduct our interviews; so our gratitude goes to Yacchan at Socrates, Inoue at Eramasa and Ta-Ko at Hawkwind. Napalm of the Seirenkyō was a great source of knowledge and allowed us to sit in on committee meetings. Extra thanks go to Shintarō at Marushin, for hosting our interviews, providing us with contacts, and supplying his own invaluable insights and experience.

We would like to thank Noriko Manabe and the 33 1/3 team for their input and confidence in us to produce this volume. Jessica Schwartz, Julia Sneeringer, Daniel Joseph and Jeff Hayton were very kind to listen to us. Daniel Milne hosted us for a workshop in Kyoto, Sara Park introduced us to many people, Till Kanudt and many others at Kyoto University gave us their time. Chikako Shimosaka and Chisako Ohara deserve special mention for helping us with the interview transcripts and persevering with our terrible Japanese skills.

On a more official note we would like to thank Kyushu University, Penn State's Asian Studies, Jewish Studies, and the Center for Global Studies, as well as Kyoto University for funding that enabled research for this project.

Finally, we would like to express our heartfelt gratitude to Kato David Hopkins, whose documentation of the Kansai music scene was an inspiration to us and remains unmatched. Unfortunately, David passed away on 18 November 2022, and we therefore dedicate this volume to his memory.

Introduction

In 1982, Kanda Takayuki, a working-class youth out of Kyoto's less affluent neighbourhoods, dropped out of high school. There was nothing unusual about this decision.[1] Kanda was one of many youths in his neighbourhood who found Japan's rigid and conformist education system too much to bear. He did not wish to continue his education and become a company salaryman. Most of his cohort found jobs in factories or joined a *bōsōzoku* (bike gang). But Kanda wished neither to join the proletariats nor to ride one of the bike gangs' customized motorcycles, waving imperial banners; he needed something else. This was not about politics or class. Although the speed of their motorcycles appealed to him, what he found repulsive about the *bōsōzoku* was their lame (*dasai*) sense of fashion, and even more so, their taste in music. He could not abide by the saccharine-filled ballad-pop songs they liked. Instead, he turned to punk, as it seemed to offer what he was looking for: a music that spoke to him, presented a way to become autonomous and provided a community of like-minded peers whom he could join. On New Year's Eve, 1982, he shaved his hair into a mohawk and dropped out of school, dedicating himself to the punk lifestyle. Kanda started to hang out around Kyoto's punk clubs, going to shows in places like Takutaku

---

[1]   Japanese names are written according to Japanese convention, surname first, followed by given name. We make exceptions if an individual works outside Japan is published in non-Asian languages or prefers to go by nickname.

or the legendary Seibu Kōdō, an event space affiliated with Kyoto University. As a 14-year-old in 1983, he and some friends attended a show by a mix of local and national acts – Masturbation, Hijōkaidan and the Stalin. This show inspired him and his friends to form their own bands, creating a new generation of hardcore punks in the vibrant Kyoto scene in which he remains a part to this day (Kanda et al. 2021).

This book captures Kanda's sociological and musical journey into punk. To do so, we map the Kyoto hardcore punk scene through the 1987 album *Don't Be Swindle* by Kanda's contemporaries, S.O.B. It is a story of a scene, place, people and sound that are not often written about in Japanese music history. The lens of loud and fast punk offers a novel way to look at Japan's ancient capital as it decentres the narrative of music production away from Tokyo; (mostly) middle-class or elite musicians, producers and record labels; and the usual focus on Kyoto as a centre of traditional elite culture. S.O.B. was a band of high school dropouts, who came out of a scene that developed from the flourishing avant-garde culture around Seibu Kōdō. In his seminal account of the 1980s Kansai music scene, David Kato Hopkins claimed that S.O.B. has one-note songs, four-note songs and occasional strange vocal intrusions that show them as 'real Osakans' (Hopkins 2015, 202). For many fans of S.O.B., the band is seen as an Osaka group. While we do not disagree with Hopkins' description of the band's sound and that Osaka was very important for S.O.B., we believe that Kyoto played an equal if not even more important role in their development.

S.O.B. was first established in Osaka in 1985 by vocalist Tottsuan (Suzuki Yoshitomo). In 1986, the band went through a full change in line-up, with fellow Osakan Fukuhara Naoto taking over on bass. The (hard) core of the band's sound

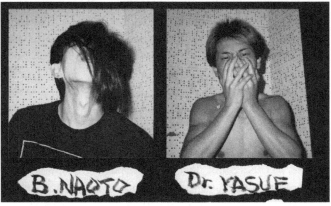

Figures 1A and 1B *S.O.B. posing on the back cover of Don't Be Swindle (courtesy of S.O.B.).*

was created when Naoto enlisted guitarist Seki Toshimi and drummer Yasue Satoshi, initially to 'help out'; they still claim to be helping out thirty-seven years later. Yasue and Seki were part of a group of Kyoto punks who had created their own hardcore sub-scene that overlapped with that of nearby Osaka. Both the people and the place of Kyoto were important in this history. S.O.B. benefitted from Kyoto's pre-existing alternative music scenes dating from the 1960s, especially Seibu Kōdō. This space, still active, has a legendary status in Japan akin to CBGBs in New York or SO36 in Berlin. Seki, Yasue, Kanda and others were trailblazers. But punks in 1987 had the freedom and indeed, the creative and physical space to act, because of the generation that came before them (whom they overtly rejected and constantly fought with). That generation had kept the flames of anarchy and autonomy burning in Kyoto.

But why *Don't Be Swindle*? And why 1987? Why not the traditional starting date of punk in 1977, with which Kyoto has rich connections? 1987 may seem a decade too late to begin a book on the growth of the punk scene, and S.O.B. may seem too obscure a band. Punk quickly transformed and evolved. Indeed, many claimed it was already dead by 1977, with bands transitioning to new wave and other genres. By 1983, the British band Cock Sparrer was lamenting the move away from the punk ethos of the original generation in their anthem, 'Where Are They Now?' (Razor Records 1983). The music magazine *Doll* claimed that the punk scene in Kansai had also become stale but was on the cusp of a revival (*Doll* 27 1983, 50). S.O.B. offers a focus to discuss this new generation of 1980s punks. They were mostly teenagers, too young to be part of the original '77 generation of Kyoto punks. Their scene created lifelong connections. Kanda, for example, formed his first band, Greed, with S.O.B.'s Naoto and currently acts as S.O.B.'s roadie. These kids took their musical cue from the evolution of punk into hardcore – a faster, more aggressive way of playing punk that was taking root in the United Kingdom and United States (Seki and Yasue 2021). According to *Flex!*, a comprehensive discography of Japanese punk, the album they produced became 'essential listening and one of the first Japanese records that you should hear and get' (Burkhard 2020).

In the second half of the 1980s, hardcore morphed into grindcore, a fusion of metal and punk, signified by distorted down-tuned guitars, overdriven bass, blast-beat drums and growling vocals. Along with their contemporaries, Napalm Death in the UK, S.O.B. were pioneers of the grindcore genre, helping to flog some life back into punk. A seminal album, *Don't Be Swindle,* had influence beyond Kansai. It showcased the band's approach to music, denoting a shift in global punk styles and winning them a national and international following. During their European tour, S.O.B. became the first Japanese band to record with the influential British DJ John Peel.[2] *Don't Be Swindle* takes the study of punk out of Kyoto and into the wider world, while providing a window onto the Kyoto scene.

Punk in history

Why tell the story of the Kyoto music scene? Although it is mostly known as a centre of traditional culture and a tourist destination, Kyoto also has a long history as a centre of alternative cultural production. Kyoto's own DIY style was born out of the praxis and infrastructure built by its fervent student movement and the artists, punks and misfits that upheld these traditions around university 'autonomous zones' and other sites throughout the city.[3] In many respects,

---

[2]   The Peel Sessions helped to launch the careers of a number of artists, such as the Undertones.

[3]   Do-It-Yourself (DIY) is a core defining feature of punk culture. Per Kevin Dunn and other punk scholars, DIY entails a rejection of the status quo and capitalist modes of cultural production. It 'provides individuals and local communities with resources for self-empowerment and political resistance' (Dunn 2016, 112, 121).

Don't Be Swindle came out of the time and place of Kyoto in the 1980s. As historians, we set out to situate the music and the people who made it within that time as a product of the historical time and space when and where it was created. We soon found that the history of punk in Kyoto to be complex and multidirectional. It intersected with the history of music, the global history of punk and related genres, the history of radicalism and student activism, and the history of Kyoto itself. But the stories of the particular scene that produced the album are mostly untold.

Studies by David Novak (2013), Hopkins (2015, 2020) and Brooke McCorkle Okazaki (2021), as well as works by punk participants (Ishiya 2020a, 2020b, 2022), have shed light on the Kansai punk scene. But overall, mainstream academic historians and sociologists of music in Japan and abroad tend to sideline Kansai and punk. Minamida Katsuya, for instance, dedicates a chapter to punk in his history of Japanese rock, yet focuses mainly on Tokyo. He mentions influential Kyoto and Kansai bands like Inu but does not differentiate these from the Tokyo scene. Minamida argues that Tokyo punk mostly reacted to the American punk scene and was more an artistic than a social expression of opposition (Minamida 2009, 150). Musically, he sees punk as a rejection of the 'new music' of bands like Happy End and singer-songwriter Arai Yumi, echoing what Michael Bourdaghs sees as a 'negation of negation' – the rejection of both commercial music and political folk music (Bourdaghs 2012, 159). Drawing on Pierre Bourdieu's theories of art in the French Second Empire, Minamida discusses this move as part of a three-way dialectical relationship. He divides the music of the 1970s into 'commercial art', 'social art' that rose in opposition to it from the left and 'pure art' that in an anti-Hegelian fashion rose not as a synthesis of the two but as a rejection of both. The latter 'claimed the right to define for itself the principles of its legitimacy' (Minamida 2015, 123–4).

Such a theory makes sense if one focuses on Tokyo. This omission of Kansai is peculiar, given Minamida's important contribution to understanding scenes as *ba* or place, which he, again drawing from Bourdieu, translates as *habitus* (Bourdaghs 2012, 114–18). According to Bourdieu, all social practice occurs in fields. The habitus provides a set of unifying principles; it organizes and articulates the position of a certain group creating a system of classification within social spaces (Bourdieu 2010, 166).

Minamida's insights connect to many punk and music scholars of 'scene', such as Andy Bennett, Ian Rogers and others who were reacting to earlier, classic work by Dick Hebdige on punk as a 'subculture' (Bennett and Rogers 2016, 5). As Kevin Dunn noted, since Hebdige's key study on punk, *Subcultures: The Meaning of Style* (1979), many scholars criticized the concept for 'ignoring participants' subjectivity, failing to do close empirical research, and being locked into a Marxist class-based analysis' (Dunn 2016, 116). Bennett and Rogers define scenes as 'entities that are both spatial and temporal, inscribed with memory and emotion and affect, [thus] we are able to recast scenes as multispatialized' (Bennett and Rogers 2016, 6). Other scholars like Martin Stokes and Marc Olson also emphasize that the interplay of space, place and emotion makes a scene or habitus (Dunn 2016, 129, 133). The main difference in the concepts used by Hebdige, the scholars of the Centre for Contemporary Cultural Studies (CCCS) and scene theory is the emphasis on class by the former and the emphasis on music and emotions in the latter. Scenes are considered as defined less by particular spaces or established standards. As Will Straw argued, a musical scene 'is that cultural space in which a range of musical practices coexist, interacting with each other within a variety of processes of differentiation, and according to widely varying trajectories of change and cross-fertilization' (Dunn 2016, 117). This more dynamic conceptualization fits better with the Kyoto scene, which remains eclectic in terms of class, gender, educational background and musical taste.

Bourdieu's concept of habitus is an influential principle in punk studies. Punk scholars have used his theories to explain the variety and vibrancy of local scenes and define the 'punk habitus' as 'social structures that provide us with mental maps for life' (Dunn 2016, 65). Habitus, like scene and subculture, is a contentious term, but it refers to the interplay of place and actions that contribute to the formation of a scene or give it distinct characteristics. The Kyoto Punk scene exemplifies this interplay, with various groups and scenes interacting with Seibu Kōdō as both a site and as a scene.

The punk habitus and its associated scene were about more than just music. The Kyoto punk scene was a dynamic interplay of physical places like Seibu Kōdō and record stores, as well as objects like cassettes and magazines, with networks of people to create a communal feeling and musical style. S.O.B. and hardcore punk emerged from Kyoto as a result of these interactions between people, physical places and objects. For clarity, we divide our analysis of the scene into two parts: the physical spaces and networks that created it, and the individuals who acted within it. The study of a scene encompasses the study of people with various personalities, motivations and dreams. Women and men, working-class punks and middle-class music students all had different experiences with the scene, as detailed in the individual biographies in Chapter 3.

Global punk/Japanese punk

The spatial differentiation of the Kyoto habitus was especially important as if there was any unifying aspect to it, it was its opposition to Tokyo. Tokyo music is often confused with Japanese music. Hopkins has argued that while Tokyo often claims the ability to define 'Japaneseness', it merely defines 'Tokyoness' for the most part, omitting spaces outside the metropole (Hopkins 2015, 45). Though still in a supposedly subordinate position in Western music, Kyoto and Kansai were historically the economic, political and cultural rivals of Tokyo. David Novak's work on the Kansai noise scene directly challenges this narrative by showing how music circulates globally without centring Tokyo, such as between Osaka and New York. For many fans, Osaka noise is Japanese noise (Novak 2013, 7).[4] There was nothing particularly nationalistic about what happened in Kyoto; apart from some right-wing bands, punks did not overly concern themselves with being Japanese. However, it is significant that unlike recent scholarship focused on African American music in Japan, the question of musicians' 'Japaneseness' in writing on the punk scene rarely comes up. The jazz musicians (Atkins 2001) and hip-hop artists (Condry 2006) had to examine their positionality as Asians engaging in genres originated by African Americans, whom they recognized as a disadvantaged racial group. The adoption, or appropriation, of these genres, particularly by middle-class Japanese, resulted in a variety of complex reactions and debates within Japanese music scenes. Punk's assimilation into Japan caused less complications. Like swing, rock and other genres the transition

---

[4] In agreement with Kato Hopkins (2020) we prefer the term 'noizu' over 'Japanoise'.

from white to Japanese performers was less problematic, even though some white American punks attempted to claim that Japanese artists (or even British ones) were appropriating punk. Unlike earlier generations of musicians, such as debates over singing in Japanese as examined by Bourdaghs, or punks in Germany who transitioned to singing in German, such questions were rarely raised in the Kyoto punk scene (Bourdaghs 2012; Hayton 2022).

Global punk typically claims to ignore racial or ethnic characteristics and fault lines. We frequently encountered this supposed punk colourblindness, which is itself a thorny issue. Similar to how noizu (noise music) was received abroad, Japanese hardcore was referred to as 'Japcore' by the US music press. This was a problematic appellation for bands like S.O.B., who saw it as derogatory and racist. Nonetheless, as Ishiya from the band Forward notes, the singling out of Japanese hardcore as 'Japcore' at least showed that the West recognized something different in the Japanese scene, and that Japanese hardcore represented, for global hardcore punk fans, a positive aspect of Japanese culture (Ishiya 2020a, 26). The term 'Japcore' may suggest that Japanese punk was a derivative of Western punk. Kyoto punks did not see it as such; indeed, the DIY ethos meant that such questions were not asked or raised. Nonetheless, punks looked to international scenes for inspiration and news. Japanese fanzines regularly featured reports on foreign scenes and the records they produced.

In the 1980s and 1990s, Japanese hardcore punk bands rarely toured abroad, and when they did, it was to the United States and Europe; it was not until the twenty-first century that they began visiting Japan's neighbours – South Korea, Taiwan and other Asian locales. This raises the issue of punk's globalization, which we will also examine. To what extent do punk networks, as described by Kevin Dunn, represent an alternative to capitalist-driven globalization? Punk scholars' descriptions of DIY networks contain an element of sentimentality. We do share these sentiments. When the Tokyo-based punk collective Irregular Rhythm Asylum (IRA) organizes trans-Asian benefits for punks imprisoned by the military regime in Myanmar, one cannot help but admire and appreciate the spirit and selflessness that drives such networks (IRA 2023). Indeed, punk is frequently described as alternative because of how the participants idealize and present their networks and practices. However, we argue that power and hierarchies still have a significant impact on how networks operate. Certain punk scenes are more 'punk' than others.

Kyoto's position as a peripheral scene is an important aspect of punk history that should be studied in depth. In our research, we draw on work by Jeff Hayton, Mirko Hall and other scholars of German and other punk scenes, who aim to decentre the overtly Anglophone world of punk scholarship (Hayton 2022, 9; Hall et al. 2018, 7). As Hall noted, Brian Cogan's *The Encyclopedia of Punk* dedicated over 75 per cent of its content to the United States and United Kingdom, and only four other countries – Japan, France, Australia and New Zealand – had any mention at all (Cogan 2006; Hall et al. 2018, 6). This situation is changing with work on punk scenes in Indonesia, Argentina, Mexico and elsewhere, showing punk's global reach and vibrancy (O'Connor 2002, 225–36; Rohrer 2014; Wallach 2014, 148–61). This is not just a matter of balancing the scholarly focus; the Kyoto scene's position on the margins was a significant factor in its formation and identity. Feelings of marginalization fed into two affective forces that shaped the Kyoto punk scene and its music: anger and a yearning for anger and abandonment.

Drawing from Andy Bennett and Ian Rogers, we analyse Kyoto punks as an 'affective community' and Seibu Kōdō as a memory space (*lieu de mémoire*; Bennett and Rogers 2016, 6). The feelings of anger and liberation offered by places like Seibu Kōdō were the affective forces that fuelled the scene. As Alan O'Connor demonstrated in his work on Washington, DC, the punk 'habitus for participants include[d] the personal and social geography' of their own city (O'Connor 2002, 227). Live venues, record stores, and hangout corners formed the geographies of memory and identity that participants invested with emotional power (Drozdzewski et al. 2016, 447–56). Participants often speak of Seibu Kōdō in particular as akin to national *lieux de mémoire* such as the Hiroshima and Nagasaki Memorial Parks – a 'temple' and 'sacred ground' for the avant-garde and music (Zwigenberg 2014). Every generation of musicians and artists invested Seibu Kōdō with myths and emotions, creating a space of freedom that simultaneously anchored the scene's identity. Seibu Kōdō would take on different 'emotional regimes', or dominant modes of emotional expression in that context, which enabled participants to embody who they imagined themselves to be and act accordingly (Reddy et al. 2010, 242).

The importance of the space and the scene touches on two additional topics. For most Kyoto residents, Seibu Kōdō likely held little significance. However, we argue that it was and continues to be important in the larger history of Kyoto and Japanese radicalism. Kyoto's punk and avant-garde scenes continued the 1960s' challenge to Japan's model of capitalist development. According to Mōri Yoshitaka (for Japan) and Jeff Hayton and others (for Germany), the DIY ethos manifests aspects that originated in the 1960s and persisted into the punk era. In addition, remnants of the 1960s scene in both countries – specifically the infrastructure and people – enabled punk to flourish in artistic spaces like Seibu Kōdō (Mōri 2009, 119). Oguma Eiji, a scholar of the 1968 generation and a participant in the Tokyo punk scene as part of the Atomic Café collective in the 1980s, remembers generational conflict between the older 30–40-year-olds and the 20-year-olds, but also that the older contingent were the main organizers of shows (Oguma 2022).

The continued presence and relevance of spaces like Seibu Kōdō and other alternative havens for radicals show a different Kyoto to the one usually studied by historians. Kyoto is often seen as 'quiet' and 'unchanging'. Thus, William Andrews mentions in his survey of radicalism and counterculture that in the 1960s, '*Even the old capital of Kyoto* saw violent protests … [but] Kyoto, *despite its elegance*, had the highest magnitude of popular disturbance per capita in the immediate post-occupation period' (Andrews 2016, 19; our emphasis). We argue that the existence of violence and protest in Kyoto should not be a surprise. In fact, Kyoto's supposed marginality as the 'old capital' (and cheap rents) made it a centre of avant-garde culture, and it should be acknowledged as such. In this viewpoint, we join a growing number of scholars who emphasize Kyoto's vibrant modern history from the Meiji Restoration onwards (Breen et al. 2020; Endō 2018; Tseng 2018).

Don't Be Swindle: **Argument and structure**

To write about *Don't Be Swindle*, we conducted oral interviews with members of S.O.B. and others from the wider Kyoto punk scene, as well as collected information from formal and informal archives in Kyoto, memoirs and other contemporary material. From this archival base, we present the first documentary history of the emergence of the scene. While relying primarily on historical methodology, we integrate different disciplinary approaches in our study, such as ethnomusicological studies of time, place, people and networks that produce scenes. At its core, the book aims at historically situating space, people and their interactions (i.e. the punk habitus of Kyoto) to answer a basic question – what leads a scene or a band to have a particular sound. We thus connect the music of *Don't Be Swindle* to the time and place that produced it. This is not a linear story. Bands are influenced by one another, of course, but this is not an old-school intellectual history which leads from Kant to Hegel (or the Clash to Fugazi) in neat, straight lines. Bands and their sounds are products of an assortment of interactions, atmospheres, moods and a habitus that includes individual creative minds and the scenes that nourish them. Thus, for the purpose of historical analysis, our chapters, somewhat artificially, separate places, people and sounds.

This book addresses the questions raised above through six chapters that are (roughly) chronologically ordered to map out the 1980s Kyoto music scene. Chapters 1 to 3 examine the emergence of the Kyoto punk scene and S.O.B.'s place in it. Chapter 1 examines the musical and cultural infrastructure laid out by the student radicals, artists and musicians who created the Seibu Kōdō free space. Chapters 2 and 3 look at the Kyoto punk scene and the people within it, including the role of gender. Most of the musicians and other producers of Japanese punk were male, especially in the hardcore scene. Recent scholarship addresses this imbalance, and while we focus on an all-male band, we acknowledge the vital contributions of Kyoto's female punks to the scene.

Chapter 4 examines the recording of the album itself and its growth out of S.O.B. members' musical and social interactions with the scene. Chapter 5 considers the reception of the album, using two S.O.B. live shows as windows into the relationship between punk and politics in the Kyoto scene in the crucial year of 1989. The year had begun with Emperor Hirohito's death, forcing the nation into silence. S.O.B. and other Kyoto punk and hardcore bands defied the silence, politicizing them and their radical noise. Chapter 6 looks beyond 1989 to S.O.B.'s interactions with global hardcore, highlighting exchanges between local and global, and between periphery and metropole.

In her discussion on British women in punk, Helen Reddington challenges the overarching myth of punk having started in 1976 and ended in 1978 with the demise of the Sex Pistols. As Reddington explains, punk, true to its anarchic nature, existed in many forms long before and after this apparent watershed; indeed, it is still a way for people and groups to express their identity, regardless of location (Reddington 2012, 1). The Kyoto punk scene of the 1980s connected to this sentiment, which still resonates with the city in many ways. While Seibu Kōdō's heyday was in the 1970s, it continues to be a centre for experimental theatre, lectures on radical politics and musical performances (Novak 2013, 109). Looking at the hardcore punk scene and its evolution through the lens of S.O.B., we shed light on an important cultural bootprint left on the city.

1 I'm a dreamer: The origins and infrastructure of the Kyoto scene (1968–80)

On 20 March 1980, the British band The Police performed to a packed audience at Seibu Kōdō. In performing there, The Police were following in the footsteps of Frank Zappa, the Stranglers and other successful international bands. These shows left quite an impression on the local music scene and were celebrated in the music press and in musicians' recollections. This time, however, the concert sparked a crisis and serious conflict. Midway through the performance, a group of people stormed the stage and the mixing desk to stop the show. They were forcibly removed by security, and several scuffles notwithstanding, the concert continued. The Police themselves had little to do with the drama that unfolded. In fact, they had no idea what was going on. In a video of the show produced by the band (that captured the energy and atmosphere of the venue), guitarist Andy Summers simply told a young interviewer, 'There were a lot of crazy people there' (The Police, 1980). These 'crazies' were members of the Seibu Kōdō liaison association, *Seibu Kōdō Renraku Kyō Shikikai*, abbreviated to *Seirenkyō*. Members of this group were incensed by what they saw as a violation of the unwritten rules of the venue. The concert organizers had supposedly deceived the Seirenkyō as to the nature of the show, brought in external security and ignored their pleas to stop the event. The event led to a crisis at the Seirenkyō, its temporary dissolution, and much debate and re-examination of the relationship of Seibu Kōdō with the commercial music scene.

The so-called Police incident proved to be the dividing line between the long 1960s and the age of punk and new wave at Seibu Kōdō. After 1980, Seibu Kōdō turned away from hosting big acts and commercial artists to turn decisively local. This change was the result of much soul-searching among local organizers and activists as to the relationship of music, politics, culture, and the rising wave of commercialization that seemed to swallow both the earlier wave of anti-establishment music and the first wave of punk in Japan. Renewed commitment to the local avant-garde and rejection of commercialization at Seibu Kōdō and other venues opened the door to the scene that gave birth to S.O.B., even though the band members were far too young to participate in these debates. They would nonetheless benefit from its outcome, as the turn away from commercialism dovetailed with the rise of local punk. Seirenkyō members were a mixture of Kyoto University students and an older generation of veterans of Japan's student-led rebellion of the late 1960s and 1970s. Punks consciously rejected both the music of that generation and its political and cultural stands. Yet as The Police incident shows and this chapter argues, the musical and cultural infrastructure created by the hippie generation and (more importantly) its DIY ethos were crucial in the establishment and maintenance of the 1980s punk scene in Kyoto, in similar ways to the punk scene in West Germany (Hayton 2014, 135). This chapter examines the Kyoto music scene before the 1980s and the history that led to the blossoming of hardcore punk in 1980. The chapter traces how the 1960s and 1970s scene laid the foundation for the structures and organizations of the city's music scene.

In August 1972, the makeshift plaza in front of Seibu Kōdō hosted the Phantom Festival (*Maboroshi no Mono Matsuri*). Crowds watched performances by legendary rock band Zunō Keisatsu (Brain Police) and other radical musicians, while the air was thick with the smell of marijuana (Itō 2022). The choice of Zunō Keisatsu, who were seen by some, probably incorrectly, to be supporters of the Japanese Red Army (JRA) faction, was not accidental (Gerteis 2021, 61). The event was partially held to commemorate 'the Lod JRA commandos that acted on behalf of the Palestine volunteer army', as well as show solidarity with the Sanrizuka struggle against the construction of the Narita Airport (Okumura 2006, 100). The so-called JRA commandos were in fact members of the Kyoto Partisan group, including two Kyoto university students, Okudaira Takeshi and Yasuda Yasuyuki. Both were killed during the terrorist attack on Lod Airport, Israel, in May 1972; the third terrorist, Okamoto Kōzō, was not from Kyoto and was captured, and an additional student had died in a separate incident. Students painted three red stars on the roof of the hall in their memory. These were the 'stars of Orion' (or stars of Tel Aviv, according to Seirenkyō's Kimura Hideki and Yamagata Kabuto), drawing on a quote from Okamoto (Kimura and Yamagata 2007, 164).[1]

---

[1] Okamoto's quote read, 'We three Red Army soldiers wanted to become Orion when we died. And it calms my heart to think that all the people we killed will also become stars in the same heavens. As the revolution goes on, how the stars will multiply!' (Steinhoff 1976, 843). *Seirenkyō* member Ishibashi Shōjirō claims this was not the case and was simply a design choice by those who painted the stars (Ishibashi 2022).

Figure 2 *Seibu kōdō has seen better days but the three stars remain prominently displayed on the roof.*

The Phantom Festival marked the watershed for Seibu Kōdō as a centre of student radicalism and avant-garde culture. Very little in that culture appealed to the later generation of punks that gave birth to S.O.B. The 1980s scene explicitly rejected the politics of the new left. As Mōri Yoshitaka argued, 1980s' punk was a break with what came before it. As one anonymous punk said, 'The so-called old left-wing and political movements were lame (*dasai*); [in the 1980s] we were doing it as a political movement in a different sense' (Mōri 2009, 121). Kanda Takayuki, among the first hardcore punks in Kyoto, likewise recalled, 'The student movement was the outlet for the energy of the young people of that time, but by our time, [the energy] was all gone. So for us, [punk] was just a part of a delinquent culture.' Kanda and his peers saw their music as a rejection of all that came before them: 'Punk … aimed at being the ultimate delinquent [culture], and it was a real counterculture with its music' (Kanda et al. 2021). Punk politics in the 1980s focused on lifestyle and rejected society. They were not aiming at building a revolutionary or utopian future. This is in accordance with Jennifer Milito Matsue's analysis of hardcore scene participants in Tokyo in the late-1990s, who were not explicitly taking socio-political stands through their music. Nonetheless, they expressed critiques of mainstream music and society (Milito Matsue 2009, 3). Kanda's generation embraced this stance and were proud to be shunned as delinquents. And they were not alone. Alienation was central to the punk experience. As Andy Bennett and Ian Rogers argued in relation to Australian punks, 'the realization of a punk identity will almost certainly involve a personal dimension linked to feelings of alienation or dissatisfaction with an experienced status quo' (Bennett and Rogers 2016, 47). For S.O.B. and their generation, the status quo included the hippie generation and its folk crusaders. While espousing few continuities in music, fashion or wider culture between the 1960s and 1980s generations, punks embraced a similar DIY ethos and occupied the same alternative cultural spaces that enabled artistic freedom. According to Ugaya Hiromu, a journalist who was a contemporaneous member of this scene, '[Both generations] were outcasts from mainstream society … although personally I wasn't interested in politics at all. Especially, in the left wing, any violent radical movement. But still, we shared a kind of sympathy [for] each other' (Ugaya 2022).

Kyoto's location on the periphery played an important role in the making of its music scene. Per Bennett and Rogers, 'periphery, due to the very fact of its "edge" status, offers opportunities for exposure to, and an absorption in, music in particularly nuanced ways; these become strongly embedded in memory as narrative threads through which individuals reflect on and explain their current investment in music'

(Bennett and Rogers 2016, 171–2). The Kyoto scene developed in this way. As Takeda Shōsaku and Saitō Shinya argued, Kyoto's free expression was often explained through its marginal location 'and distance from the entertainment industry' (Saitō and Takeda 2020, 90). As Itō Kimio recalled, 'Kyoto was far from Tokyo, so even if something became popular in Kyoto, agents in Tokyo would not immediately come and get it. If it became popular in Tokyo, it [i.e., commodification] would happen immediately' (Itō 2022). Within Kyoto, Seibu Kōdō was a 'memory place', often spoken about in quasi-religious terms, which anchored participants' personal and musical identities. Okumura Hidemaru, who was active in the Kyoto folk scene, remembered Seibu Kōdō as 'a radical and mysterious area, which was at the center of everything, a cathedral-like structure with black roof' (Okumura 2006, 100). Similarly, at the height of the first wave of punk, a visiting critic described the scene in the place as 'groups of young men in long coats and women with flamboyant makeup and messy hair, all dressed in a Japanese-English style … [gathered at] a large wooden arc-shaped building that looked like a temple with a curved black roof' (*Asahi Shinbun* 19 January 1980).

The black, curved roof with its Japanese traditional style was often attributed to the supposed origin of the building as 'an "annex" to the Kyoto Imperial Palace during the accession of Emperor Hirohito to the throne in 1928, [which] was later sold to Kyoto University and reconstructed as an auditorium in 1937' (*Shūkan Shinchō*, 20 April 1978). Given its status as a mecca of rebellious youth and symbol of anti-imperialism, such an exalted origin story seems appropriate, but in fact, it is only an urban legend. The hall was designed by Ōkura Saburō and Takeda Goichi, who designed many buildings on the Kyoto University campus in the 1930s (*Kensetsu Tsūshin Shinbun* 25

November 2010). Originally completed in 1937 as a martial arts hall of Kyoto University, it was part of a bigger complex that included some of the first buildings in Japanese imperial universities designated for student clubs (*Kyoto Daigaku Shinbun* 6 February 1936). In preparation for its opening, Seibu Kōdō was praised as 'by far the most splendid in the country' (*Kyoto Daigaku Shinbun* 20 June 1936). Martial arts were a central part of student life in the militarist Japan of 1937. But after the Second World War, the building was repurposed as a movie theatre, and this shift away from martial arts to the creative arts was hailed as a manifestation of a new era of freedom. The hall was now 'a modern place where movies are screened, despite its old-fashioned appearance' (*Kyoto Daigaku Shinbun* 15 May 1950).

Film and student film clubs, as well as theatre groups, continued to play a significant role in the hall. But as the 1950s gave way to the 1960s, radical students, in collaboration with the film and other cultural associations, brought new kinds of music and art into Seibu Kōdō. Institutions like the jazz, rock, folk, and go-go *kissa* (listening cafes) and live-music venues like Honyaradō adjacent to Dōshisha University became spaces of 'experimental autonomy' (*jitai no taiken*) for students and activists (Makita 2022). Performance spaces like Honyaradō and Jittoku (one of Kyoto's oldest-running concert venues) created open atmospheres where one could experiment with new forms of dance and music, like butoh and newer forms of folk (Saitō and Takeda 2020, 97). The experimental atmosphere also led to novel forms of organization. The AFL (associated folklorist) collective of musicians, for instance, put together 'dime concerts' that played in public outdoor spaces that abounded in Kyoto, such as temples and shrines (Saitō and Takeda 2020, 95, 97). Self-styled folk guerrillas from

Kansai formed impromptu music and protest groups to sing songs around train stations and raise money for the anti-war cause. This mixture of politics and cultural expression led to the occupation of Seibu Kōdō in the late 1960s and its rise as the most important centre for counterculture in Kyoto.

During massive demonstrations around Kyoto in April 1969, Kyoto University students occupied the main lecture halls on campus. They held a series of concerts under the name *bari-sai* (barricade festival), celebrating 'the world that only we inside the barricades know' (Bari-sai Schedule, 1969). Dōshisha University held concurrent events under the name, 'Barricade a Go-Go'. Both events featured the legendary rock band Hadaka no Rarīzu (Les Rallizes Dénudés), whose free-form, explosive style of distorted guitars caused quite a lot of confusion. Kimura Hideki recalled that the 'posers did not quite understand' Les Rallizes' brand of psychedelic rock. Headed by Mizutani Takashi and made up of Dōshisha University students, the band prided itself on its musical and artistic freedom. Kimura also remembered the barricade festival as controversial because 'men were kissing each other and there was a lot of mayhem'. The free-for-all was criticized by political activists, who complained to Kimura, 'What the hell does this have to do with the struggle?' (Kimura 1980a, 15).

That last comment points to the friction between the politically minded (and more austere) student activists and the culture groups that saw free expression rather than revolutionary violence as their main direction. The concert and accompanying political actions occasioned the final takeover by the students and the making of Seibu Kōdō into a 'liberated zone' (*kaihō-ku*; *Shūkan Shinchō*, 20 April 1978) – a status made concrete by the painting of the roof (one of several such occasions) and the Phantom Festival (Okumura 2006, 100).

Kimura dubbed the festival as the 'funeral procession of the 1960s' (Kimura 1980a, 15). These events of 1969 – and even more so, the *Fuck '70* Festival and events commemorating the founding of Mojo West at Seibu Kōdō the following year – saw the split between political and cultural movements.

Kimura, along with Uchida Yūya, established the Mojo West events at Seibu Kōdō, but they were ambivalent about the student movement. The feeling was mutual, as in 1969. After Mojo West featured PYG (a band composed of members from commercial group-sounds acts the Tempters, the Spiders and Kyoto's the Tigers), 'the anti-establishment students in Kyoto accused Mojo West of being a front for commercialization' and for selling out 'Seibu Kōdō [as the] symbol of radicalism' (Kimura and Yamagata 2007, 169). Kimura, Uchida and their faction in the Seirenkyō, however, were more interested in free expression rather than politics. Komatsu Tatsuo, one of the founders of the Seirenkyō and Mojo West, saw Seibu Kōdō as 'not just a place that sought [revolutionary] freedom, but a new order, a new relationship, autonomy, and responsibility' (Komatsu 1987, 247). For Kimura the *Fuck '70* festival was a start of a 'boom of youth culture in Kyoto' with Seibu Kōdō at its centre (Kimura 1980b, 2). As a former activist recalled, with the student movement at an impasse and rapidly devolving into violence, students turned to counterculture. Seibu Kōdō was an important space 'that had power to overturn conventions, maintain the spirit [of the 1960s] and show the difference between a tiny minority and mass consumption society' (Mojo West Chronicle, n.d.).

Mojo West, however, walked a fine line between commercialization and countercultural antagonism. The venue certainly maintained its radical credentials. Although the police usually kept themselves off the premises, they raided the offices of Seirenkyō several times under the suspicion that proceeds from shows went towards JRA activities (Kimura 1980b, 3). These raids, combined with its hosting events such as a marijuana symposium, added to the hall's cultural capital of radicalism and cool, turning it into one of the most important venues of the 1970s (*Shūkan Shinchō*, 20 April 1978). Performing at Seibu Kōdō, Kimura recalled unapologetically, 'became defined as a gateway to success in the rock world' (Kimura 1980b, 3).

Kyoto's unique features and scene led to new kinds of music and experimentation. New venues like Drugstore were incubators for the birth of noise and punk music in Kyoto. Drugstore and the noise scene it nurtured, in a similar fashion to Seibu Kōdō, were the products of both regional and 'transnational circuitry' of music, which bypassed Tokyo and connected straight to New York (Novak 2013, 15). The birth of noise and punk in Kyoto are difficult to separate. October 1978 was the occasion of the first punk show at Seibu Kōdō by local band SS, followed by a tour stop of Tokyo punk bands under the label Tokyo Rockers. The blend of the local and global is reflected in the comments of Shinoyan, founder of SS: 'The SS were not trying to copy foreign bands but were positioning themselves as local representatives of an international movement while still trying to create their own distinct image' (Hopkins 2015, 70). Whether they intended it or not, the SS are often cited as one of the world's first hardcore punk bands, although the extent of their influence is debatable: they broke up in 1979 and had no releases until 1984 (Burkhard 2018). Bands like INU, the Drugstore-based Hijōkaidan and Aunt Sally were starting a new genre in Kyoto dubbed no-wave, which included both what we will now call noise and punk. Inspired by punk, the new music was radical and experimental and not at all superficial. The music was hard to define and hard to swallow, with Hijōkaidan becoming especially infamous for their shocking stage act, in which they urinated and threw slabs of raw meat and garbage at the audience.

For the Kansai no-wave, Seibu Kōdō was an indispensable space. In their planning notes for a May 1979 concert, Hijōkaidan noted that Seibu Kōdō is the 'the only place that absolute freedom of expression can be had, and where costs were low or nonexistent. [Especially] for those of us who cherish live performances ... Seibu Kōdō is the best place for minor artists who have but a few chances to present their works and activities in and where they can express themselves freely'. Other venues did not present such an opportunity (Hopkins 2020, 108). Indeed, other locations did not accept or restricted no-wave artists. One venue, Circus Circus, restricted punk shows to Mondays, and others banned punk completely (Hopkins 2015, 96). Seibu Kōdō only charged maintenance fees and was open to almost anyone (although the council needed to approve all shows). Furthermore, the ethos of the place matched the attitude of the no-wave artists. As David Kato Hopkins pointed out, in 1978 'the Kansai No Wave Tour of Tokyo was self-consciously set up from the beginning as a kind of confrontational theatre, where the "real" punks of Kansai would aggressively show those Tokyo posers what real punk was' (Hopkins 2015, 96). This was an attitude that the older generation could understand: after the decline of the Shinjuku scene in the 1970s, they had held Kyoto to be where the real counterculture was made.

But maintaining the hall was a costly business. Repeated fires and the deteriorating state of the building led to many expenses. Live shows were also expensive. A 1979 report on the hall, for instance, featured an interview with council member Tsushima Ryōsuke, who said that the Seirenkyō 'is 150,000 yen in the red for an upcoming show and had to pawn its TV and Mahjong tiles' to cover expenses. The report also interviewed many concertgoers and others around Kyoto, as well as covering preparations for the 1980 New Year's concert (a tradition at Seibu Kōdō). The issue was not just money. At the end of the 1970s, with the radical student movement receding along with some of the vigour of the Kyoto cultural scene, the atmosphere was a mixture of hope and despair. Hayashi Shin, an author in the fanzine *Playguide*, said that Seibu Kōdō's performances were a rarity that 'exists only in Kyoto', as 'the student independence movement failed everywhere in the 1970s, but continues to exist only in Kyoto's Seibu Kōdō'. On the other hand, he lamented, 'only a few of us remember the season of struggle at the university'. The council itself gave the 1980 concert the name REVO 80 (Revolution 1980), with the slogan, 'Let's build a new and unique youth culture to break away from the mood of the 1970s and usher in the 80s' (*Asahi Shinbun* 19 January 1980). The feeling that Seibu Kōdō needed a generational reboot was widespread. The need for funding on one hand and the decline of the counterculture on the other brought more and more foreign and domestic acts to the hall. By the time of the Police incident, the stage had been set for a complete transformation of the site.

The Police incident made national headlines, with the *Mainichi* newspaper reporting that 'critics are now asking where the tradition of free concerts at Seibu Kōdō has gone, free not only in the sense of free of charge but as a [space] of liberation. The independent management system of this "liberated zone," which had served continuously for twenty years, seems to have reached a turning point' (*Mainichi Shinbun* 22 February 1980). The incident led to numerous debates in the Kyoto scene regarding the connections between commercialism, music, counterculture and the place of Seibu Kōdō. These debates – about the place of counterculture within a capitalist system, the role of artists in politics and the relationship between generations of artists and activists, and Seibu Kōdō's station within these systems – brought to light the theoretical and political difficulties that countercultural scenes faced in capitalist societies; they precipitated the end of big concerts at Seibu Kōdō and renewed its focus on the local scene. According to Seirenkyō member Aono Sō, 'the problems caused by this performance were a major turning point in the history of the venue … and led [us] eventually to exclude overtly commercial activities and use it as a place for free expression' (Koga 2022, 141).

Kanhō, Seibu Kōdō's zine, published a special edition in April 1980 asking, 'What relationship should Seibu Kōdō have with the music industry?' The answer, it appeared, was none. Participants in the debate, mostly performers in the space from the older generation, agreed that Seibu Kōdō should return to presenting more local acts and 'have more horizontal connections and dialogues'. The state of punk and new wave, widely regarded as a sell-out by both old and new participants, provided an important backdrop for the debates. Seirenkyō members accused music companies as villains exploiting Seibu Kōdō's anti-establishment, 'dirty, shabby, shady, and scary' atmosphere to promote foreign and domestic bands. This is the nature of the industry, as 'capital [always] seeks to monopolize all information and means of communication. Monopolies are especially easy to form in the music industry because the mediums are records and broadcasting, both of which require significant amounts of money'. In the case of punk, 'what capital can tolerate was turned into a commodity and what it cannot, it suppressed' (*Kanhō*, April 1980 [2:2], 2). An unnamed Seirenkyō member (writers for *Kanhō* rarely identified themselves) wrote that the media called it 'the "world's Seibu Kōdō" and a "rock temple"', but the 'reality is that Seibu Kōdō is a broken-down building with no proper facilities'. Thus, the council had to compromise and use 'the capitalists who wanted to use the "rock atmosphere" of Seibu Kōdō … to capture their consumers'. Punks and others criticized the council also guilty of such compromise, as 'bands with an anti-establishment "mood" and radical cultural figures with a radical "vibe" began to "sell" their wares without even realizing it'. Echoing wider criticism beyond Japan, the anonymous author wrote, 'that "punk" was turned into a slogan for "new wave" shows the insignificance of the movement and the size of its "enemy"'. Music is 'never free of politics', while 'only singing political songs' does not 'make you political' (*Kanhō*, August 1980 [2:3], 6).

Such understanding reinforced a sense that real political change was in the creation of alternative spaces and lifestyles. As *Playguide*'s Takenaka Iso wrote, 'The Police Incident reminded us of the threat of capital and power to our musical and cultural situation … I take this as a catalyst for a renewed awareness of our music, our culture, and our way of life' (*Kanhō*, November 1980 [2:4], 8). That such 'a culture and way of life' could thrive and resist the onslaught of commercialization was largely thanks to the existence of Seibu Kōdō as an anchor for a vibrant Kyoto scene. Although S.O.B. and other punks had little in common with the intellectuals and artists that patronized Seibu Kōdō (and did not overly concern themselves with issues of capitalism), the two groups shared a common belief in the DIY principle. Like the cooperation between punk and cultural luminaries like Alfred Hilsberg in

Germany, 'the DIY principle was the primary means of realizing the punk revolution'. Like the *Seirenkyō* members of the early 1980s, Hilsberg 'believed that punk can return the promise cf revolution that was lost' (Hayton 2014, 136, 137). And similarly, members of the 1960s generation in Germany, Japan and beyond were the ones who supplied the spaces and infrastructure that made punk in Kyoto possible. Seibu Kōdō was central to this quest for revolution. It paralleled what Alan O'Connor observed in US punk venues that showed 'a solid commitment to benefit shows for community institutions in the poorer part of the city … and the rejection of the corporate rock industry' (O'Connor 2002, 227). Such similarities were not accidental, as Seibu Kōdō was drawing on global models and was part of a transnational punk scene. In this global network, it followed the hippies' footsteps. The modes of music and cultural circulation that were born and developed in Kyoto in the 1960s and 1970s were repurposed and used by the no-wave and punk bands that came after them. And, with the final rejection of Tokyo-based commercial music, Seibu Kōdō now opened up to a new generation of local but globally oriented musicians to claim the space as their own.

2 Speed my way: The organization of the wider Kyoto punk scene, 1977–86

In 1983, a group of young punks, including future members of S.O.B., began regularly attending live shows at Seibu Kōdō and other venues around Kyoto and Osaka. Yasue Satoshi, Imai Kazuhiro and Kanda Takayuki were in eighth grade or had already dropped out of school at that time. Kanda recalls that 'when I started going to Seibu Kōdō, I was really shocked' (Kanda et al. 2021). One of the first shows he saw was a performance at Seibu Kōdō on 17 September 1983 featuring the Stalin and Hijōkaidan, organized by the Kyoto-based Beat Crazy collective. The Stalin were one of Japan's pioneering punk bands, formed by Endō Michirō in 1980. By 1983, however, he had grown tired of the punk formula and was looking for something more extreme. He thus joined the Kyoto group Hijōkaidan for a performance that incorporated audience intimidation, nudity, bodily fluids and violence, for which the noise legends were known. As usual, Hijōkaidan featured a somewhat improvised cast (with Hayashi Naoto replacing regular member Miwakawa Toshiji). Jojo Hiroshige and the rest of the band, combined with the Stalin as Stā-Kaidan, delivered their usual act. David Kato Hopkins, who first came to Kyoto in the late 1970s and became an integral part of the scene, reported that the show 'was thoroughly transgressive, violent and disgusting which is what everyone came to see' (Hopkins 2020, 218). The band threw dead fish, meat and other refuse at the audience, and the combined Stā-Kaidan group acted in the most shocking way possible. The young punks were duly impressed. Kanda recalled, 'they had blue sheets all over the place … and had to chain the door so that people couldn't get out' (Kanda et al. 2021). According to Jojo Hirsohige of Hijōkaidan, the show attracted over a thousand people, and many, like Tottsuan, were inspired to form bands (Hiroshige 2013, 35).

In reminiscing about the show and their teenage fascination with it, Imai remembered thinking, 'I don't know what it is, but there's a woman urinating … inside, [we thought to ourselves] so let's go see it. Titties? Let's go see. What was it? I don't know' (Kanda et al. 2021). Beside rumours of bare-chested women peeing on stage (which problematically brought up attendance), Kanda and others likely learned about the show via the 'Beat Crazy Topic' section of the *Pelican Club* zine. This zine reported on this and upcoming shows by the Continental Kids, a key band of the Beat Crazy collective, which were 'going up to Tokyo to represent the Kansai scene with their energetic acts' (*Pelican Club*, August 1983, 49). After the show, the young punks could listen to the act, which was recorded and distributed on cassette tape under the simple heading, *Stā-Kaidan Kyoto Daigaku Seibu Kōdō 1983.8. 27 Live* (*Sutārin × hijōkaidan*). Unlike the records of the 1970s, cassettes were cheap and circulated widely among individuals and around scenes. Affordable cassettes, together with new networks like Beat Crazy and new venues, constituted the scene from which S.O.B. emerged.

The young Kanda and Imai were initiated into a punk scene that was already unique and vibrant. The punk scene in Kyoto defies simple definition. As with most other punk scenes, even to call it a punk scene does it an injustice, as the scene was not defined by the music alone and was more about attitudes and affect, namely anger, defiance and fun. Noise bands like Hijōkaidan and venues like Drugstore were also part of the punk scene. Likewise, at Seibu Kōdō, radical dance and theatre troupes shared space, ideas and organizational apparatus with the Beat Crazy punk collective, whose founding member Shinoyan vehemently denied being punk at all. Musically, 'Japanese Punk did not necessitate a rejection of old wave or prog rock unlike in the UK' (Hopkins 2015, 37). There was much flexibility and alteration of styles, with many punks listening to 'difficult jazz' and new wave. 'Even the hardcore bands', Hopkins recalled, 'they start to thrash away, but the song would break down and they would just be thrashing. Hmm. So is it still hardcore? Yeah. Or has it changed into something else?' (Hopkins 2022). Kyoto was too small to have significant borders among different musical styles. Bide of Ultra Bide, for instance, had an older mentor from Datetenryū (a progressive rock band and Mojo West regular), and Bide considered himself a progressive rock musician, even though he mostly played punk (Hopkins 2022). The scene called itself 'Kansai no wave', and scene members did not see contradictions in mixing genres. This contrasted with the German punk scene. in which *Kunstpunks* and hardcore punks, who often did not even consider themselves as part of the same scene, clashed over appearance, politics and different musical styles (Hayton 2022, 125).

Punks also stood out by the clothes they wore, which made them instantly recognizable to each other. Within the scene, fashion further divided and identified subgroupings. Fashion was an important factor for S.O.B. Many Japanese bands were influenced by British punk style. Shortly after they came onto the scene, S.O.B. found the leather jackets, boots and studs of punk to be too sartorially uniform, and they sought something different. Imai and others adopted skateboard fashion; their go-to look became T-shirts, converse trainers, and later, vans, while always carrying a skateboard. Skateboard fashion was a visual signifier that made the band stand out and placed them apart from previous punk generations. While skateboarding had taken off as an outsider culture in the United States by the mid-1980s, it was then still regarded as a mere child's toy in Japan. Older peers had criticized Yasue and Imai for adopting skateboard fashion in their previous band, Seltic Frost (not to be confused with the Swiss metal band Celtic Frost) (Seki et al. 2021). Like children's manga for 1960s youth, who read them as a form of rebellion, juvenile skater style rebelled against an overly uniform punk culture.

While S.O.B. stood out among the 'groups of young men in long coats and women with flamboyant makeup and messy hair' that frequented punk venues, they still felt a sense of belonging and freedom in them. The biggest and most important venue for the second wave of punks was Seibu Kōdō, a continuation of its role in earlier waves. Kanda called it 'our Budōkan' (Kanda et al. 2021).[1] Tamura Takahisa from the Cockney Cocks (inspired by British football-hooligan-style oi punk), a Beat Crazy regular, said that while his band liked playing in Takutaku and other small venues, 'Kyoto University's Seibu Kōdō was the holy ground for punk' (*panko no seichi*; Tamura 2020). But Seibu Kōdō could not be used

---

[1] Nippon Budōkan first became a major concert venue when it hosted the Beatles in 1966, and like Seibu kōdō was and still is a martial arts venue being purpose built for the 1966 Olympics.

on a daily basis. It was too big, and the procedures for using it required time. An ever-changing network of live venues, rehearsal spaces, record stores and rock cafes sustained the scene. The two most important spaces after Seibu Kōdō were Circus Circus, next to Ginkakuji (the Silver Pavilion Temple) and the Avix (pronounced a-bi-e-k-ku-su), which was next to the intersection of Gojō and Karasuma streets. Circus Circus, which was later named CBGB (after the famous New York City music venue and signifying its changed attitude towards punk), was a small venue in a basement. According to Wada Ryōichi from Vampire, the booker was a friend and invited punk groups from Tokyo and Kyoto to perform there (Wada 2022). Another important venue was Osaka's Eggplant. Both the Eggplant, being especially friendly for hardcore, and Avix, which did not have a liquor license and thus could admit underage punks, played an especially important role in S.O.B.'s development.

Record stores and rehearsal spaces, which often doubled as both, were also important in Kyoto's punk map. As anyone who was initiated into punk in the 1980s could tell you, record stores selling foreign magazines were 'a physical and psychic space to escape to' (Hopkins 2015, 17). Record stores were a magical portal where one connected to places like New York or London 'where things happened' and where you felt at home, away from the dreariness and social conformity around your particular geography. Jūjiya on Sanjō was the most important store in Kyoto, along with Riverside Records on Kawaramachi. Jūjiya was the place to go if you wanted to hear punk. Per Hopkins, 'I don't know what their connection was and whether they were just reading in *NME* and ordering what sounded good, [but] they had access to lots of [stuff]. Mainly British records that we wouldn't see anyplace else.' Hopkins further recalled, 'Hirakawa Shin worked there. He was a very influential person because he cared about his customers, and he knew you and said, "You're going to like this one" and recommended stuff to you' (Hopkins 2022). Hirakawa, a musician who worked with Shonen Knife, was one of the 'older people' who introduced Wada and others to new albums and music from abroad; he 'would tell us that this just came out, or that this is a new thing' (Wada 2022).

Record stores worked in tandem with magazines and zines, which were also available in venues. Nakamura Shintarō (of the bands Anti-Spectacle and First Alert), remembered going to Jūjiya, 'which had a lot of American hardcore', after reading record-store ads in *Doll* magazine that showed what was in stock: 'I'd see it, and I'd call them right away, or I'd mail order them, or I'd just go to the record shop.' According to Imai, 'one [of us] would buy [the magazine] and make a list', and they would get what they could. *Rock Magazine, Fool's Mate* and *Doll* were Tokyo-based, nationally distributed magazines. Kyoto punks also had access to San Francisco magazine *Maximum Rocknroll* (MRR) via Felix Havoc, who wrote hardcore reviews for it; he was among the older folk who went abroad and returned with magazines and records. *Doll* translated articles from *MRR* and published them in the magazine. David Kato Hopkins was a full-time punk cultural agent and circulator, who helped Hijōkaidan, Boredoms, Zeni Geva and other bands get US coverage. As already mentioned, Imai and Kanda also recalled exchanging cassettes, either of taped live shows for Japanese bands or other music, as being very important in the scene (Kanda et al. 2021). The interaction between different generations and groups of punks was an important feature of the Beat Crazy collective.

Music collectives were a long-standing feature of the Kyoto scene since the folk-guerrilla days; other collectives included the EP4 collective for early electronic and industrial music and others for 'ethnic music' (Mōri 2022).[2] The Beat Crazy collective, which was formed in 1981, was 'basically a punk union' that managed the scene (Mōri 2022). The core of the collective consisted of Ishibashi, Shinoyan, Ultra Bide, Ranko of Sperma and Wada Ryōichi of Vampire. Wada later turned it into a label, pressing several 7-inch recordings of Kyoto-based bands. The large presence of university students in Kyoto was important, as it gave the collective access to the Seirenkyō (of which Wada and others were members) and to other school festivals and cultural events that students 'could get a budget from the school to put on shows. They could share this with their friends. Beat Crazy were sort of at the center of those exchanges' (Hopkins 2022). Kanda argued that 'without Beat

Figure 3 *Seki's (centre) pre-S.O.B. band the Bones performing at a 1985 Beat Crazy Event inside Seibu kōdō (photo courtesy of Minamitsuji 'Babi' Akihiro).*

---

[2] Folk guerrilla refers to the folk music street performances of the 1960s that were often political in nature. The phenomenon originated in the Kansai region.

Crazy, the 1980s music scene in Kyoto, centred around Seibu Kōdō, probably would not have existed. Many young punks sent demo tapes (to Beat Crazy), and it became a bit of a status symbol among the band members at the time' to belong to Beat Crazy (Kanda et al. 2021).[3]

Beat Crazy also had their own rehearsal space, a club room at the Kyoto University Light Music Club, which was connected to the Seirenkyō (Seki et al. 2021). Ishibashi called the space (which had no official name) the 'Rock-a-Go-Go Club', after the series of events that Beat Crazy ran at Seibu Kōdō and other places, which gave many bands their start. According to Wada, 'Shinoyan suggested that we start it' (Wada 2022). After the SS broke up, Shinoyan and drummer Isono formed the Continental Kids and founded Beat Crazy. The presence of Shinoyan, Ishibashi and older punks at the events aided the formation of younger bands like S.O.B., which comprised the second and third generations of punk. According to Ishibashi, 'many bands, even non-university students, formed bands and practiced there, so there was a sudden increase in the number of bands [that now] had places to practice' (Ishibashi 2022).

Seki mentioned that before Seibu Kōdō, which itself did not feature hardcore bands until 1984 or so, the 'music club room' was a place where 'they could play every week' (Seki et al. 2021). In this 'mini-Seibu Kōdō', everyone was welcome, and bands played small, rowdy sessions, rehearsed and recorded (Wada 2022). According to Ishibashi, 'Very few college students came. The people who came were junior-high and high-school students who were really soaked in punk (*panku dzuke*)' (Ishibashi 2022). The audience included Kanda Takayuki, who by

---

[3] Beat Crazy was an inspiration for an art collective named Art Crazy, which shows its significance (*Pelican Club,* 1 June 1983, 48).

then had formed his first band, Greed, with future S.O.B. bassist Naoto. Beat Crazy supported them and booked them to play at Seibu Kōdō; one of the earliest existing recordings of S.O.B. is from a Seibu Kōdō event in March 1986. Beat Crazy used local punks to promote shows, sell tickets and work the door. The collective attracted punks from across Kansai to their events. Tottsusan and Cherry from the band Zouo worked in security at Seibu Kōdō when GBH from the UK toured Japan (*MRR* 338, July 2011).

A 1983 report on a Kansai tour, as related by Chitose of the Comes, captures the atmosphere of the scene – the misogyny, camaraderie, unique creativity and freedom that was afforded by the Kyoto scene. In Kyoto, the Comes played with Sperma and other Beat Crazy acts in Jittoku, followed by shows in Circus Circus and a mini-show at Rock-a-Go-Go with OXZ and others. *Doll* reported that 'there was a session band consisting of members of the Continental Kids, and [then] the Comes played at the end … The room was filthy. There were roaches, maggots, and a broken-down fan that was about to catch fire.' Yet the atmosphere was amazing, a 'midsummer wonder', and the show felt 'like a family reunion'. Chitose said the band stayed in Seibu Kōdō itself and used Shinoyan's old car to get around and get food. It was hot and humid, and they even had a chance to go to the beach. When they played Circus Circus on 30 July, 'It was an all-night concert and started at midnight. We played at the top of the bill, and it was pretty exciting.' Chitose praised the performances of Vampire and Continental Kids. By the end of the night when she was listening to one of the Kyoto bands, 'I was so moved that I almost burst into tears' (*Doll* 17 August 1983, 30–1).

On the other hand, she also recalled 'there was this weird, creepy foreigner at the front, puffing on a cigarette and checking me up with a smug look on his face' (*Doll,* 17 August 1983, 31). Foreigners were not the only ones who gave her unwanted attention. Chitose and other women punks suffered from sexual harassment. A *Pelican Club* report on an earlier Comes show said, 'the crowd was really into Chitose's high-pitched voice', but the men were 'trying really hard to look up Chitose's skirt'. The same report interviewed punks who said they had come to the show because they had heard there was 'a beautiful female vocalist with beautiful legs' and that they 'were very interested in her' (*Pelican Club* June 1983, 60). As discussed further in Chapter 3, this was a common experience for women punks in Kyoto and the larger Kansai scene.

Hardcore punk was overall a male domain. Its anger and tension had the rough edge associated with rebellious masculinity. As an anonymous punk told *Pelican Club* in 1983, 'punk is, to some extent, driven by a sense of anxiety and tension that the world may collapse a minute from now, and the roughness that arises from this is what makes it so appealing' (*Pelican Club* March 1983, 49). Women had to find their place within the roughness and violence of mosh pits and cramped show spaces. As second-wave feminism and the feminine voice were often associated with the 1960s folk movement, punk and its rejection of the voice and aesthetic of its predecessors implicitly rejected feminism (Reddington 2012, 113). Despite this difficult terrain, female punks found liberation in embracing punk attitudes and aesthetics. In the stifling, neo-conservative environment of the early 1980s, punk bands eased the way to rebellion for Japanese teenage girls who wanted to rebel against their homes and parents (Ugaya 2022). As Chitose's account makes clear, punk had the potential to be emancipating and exciting for women. Rohrer Ingo points out that 'the practices and ideologies' of camaraderie and friendship hold scenes together. These practices can transcend the local scene and expand into the global scene (Ingo 2014, 206). When S.O.B. went abroad, they shared values and feelings that connected them with punks across the globe. In Kyoto, the scene was made up of personal networks and long-standing sentiments regarding musical spaces and their communities. As Allan O'Connor pointed out, punk scenes 'should be situated within a *habitus* that includes the personal and the social geography of the city'. Notably, O'Connor also mentions an 'understated emphasis on spirituality' as an element of the scenes he studied (O'Connor 2002, 227). A similar phenomenon occurred in Kyoto, especially Seibu Kōdō, as shown by its repeated references as a holy ground. Beat Crazy was not just a punk union; it was a family and a community. The live venues and physical spaces of the punk map were anchors of identity and memory, around which punks weaved the networks and friendships that sustained the scene.

3 Look like devil: Who are the punks?

This chapter looks at the punk habitus around which S.O.B. formed, showing how the punks' organization and structure capitalized on the networks established by Beat Crazy around Seibu Kōdō. Unlike the original punk generation of 1977, most teenage punks who came of age in the mid-1980s were not university-educated. There were interactions and clashes between university students and local punks in the shared spaces of the city. These punks were very young: the members of S.O.B. were still teenagers when they recorded *Don't Be Swindle*. Hardcore punk bands also constituted a male-dominated scene; nonetheless, there were vital female characters who partially redressed the gender imbalance. Despite clashes around gender and class, the scene also created opportunities, affording autonomy to women and working-class youths. Beat Crazy provided support for the new generation of punks in the region, inviting hardcore bands to play their events from 1984. Seibu Kōdō was a good venue for young bands to play, although as Seki noted, the Seirenkyō was always a pain to get past, and the place was a 'total mess' (Seki 2021).

Hardcore shows were marked by overtly macho violence and the predominance of patriarchal Japanese masculine identities (Overell 2016, 252). Many female musicians in Kyoto gravitated towards new wave bands such as OXZ or more standard punk rock such as Sekiri, who were perhaps Beat Crazy's most successful band. Teenage skateboarders who'd dropped out of all-male high schools were putting together these hardcore shows – a circumstance that reinforced male dominance. Nonetheless, there were some standout female denizens of the scene. One female performer was Sachi of the band Brain Death – a band that was a staple at Eggplant and released an EP via Selfish Records. Another example was Yamai 'Tom' Kumiko, the Osaka-based female hardcore artist whom S.O.B. commissioned to design the cover of their second album, *What's the Truth?* Tom was a key artist of the 1980s Kansai hardcore scene, having done cover art and flyers for the band Outo among others; Outo's bass player, Tunk, was in the original S.O.B. lineup. While her nickname Tom came from her resemblance to one of the Thompson Twins, it also masked her gender (*Zero Magazine 2*: 108).

The beating heart of the Kyoto scene was undoubtedly Ranko – the godmother of Kyoto punk, who Wada called 'the key figure' of the scene. Ranko had moved to Kyoto from Hiroshima in pursuit of a good music scene (Wada 2022). According to Ishibashi, as many other music scenes in Japan were increasingly rigidly fixed within a genre, she and the community found it refreshing that Beat Crazy booked a wide variety of acts, creating opportunities for mixing bands of different styles who would otherwise never have interacted with one another (Kanda et al. 2021). Ishibashi also said, 'Ranko was putting everything together. She was the weight of everything. No one would go against her, and [everyone] listen to what she had to say' (Ishibashi 2022). Much of her presence, per Ishibashi, was 'because she was the oldest. But she took very good care of them (young punks). So, if a young punk kid said he didn't have any money, she would give him money or something. She was a very caring older sister. She was also very powerful.' For Kanda, Ranko seemed like a mother figure;

'She did a great job of bringing together [people from] various genres', he continued, 'and from our point of view, she created an opportunity for us to get together with bands that we otherwise wouldn't have gotten to know' (Kanda et al. 2021). Likewise, Tamura of the Cockney Cocks recalled that Ranko gave him his first chance at the scene. 'Ranko said, "I don't know what kind of punk oi is, but your enthusiasm has won me over, so why don't you give it a try?"' She called a few days later and told him that she had arranged for a gig at Takutaku. Later, Ranko asked him to release a record on the Beat Crazy label (Tamura 2020).

Performances by Ranko and other women bands 'shook the Kyoto scene' (Tamura 2020). As male performers greatly outnumbered female ones in the 1980s punk scene, sexism and misogyny were rampant. Beat Crazy's magazine often featured interviews in which male punks were asked what kind of girls they liked, to which they, including Lemmy (Execute), answered 'cute middle-school girls' (*Pelican Club* 1 April 1983: 52). Male punks also referred to female punk musicians like Sekiri and Shonen Knife as cute girls (Tamura 2020). Women punks reacted to this environment in several ways. Shonen Knife repurposed cuteness as a subversive way to undermine the male-centredness of the punk world (McCorkle Okazaki 2021). Some female band musicians like Tom masked their gender. Still others like Ranko and Chitose deployed their sexuality to shock the audience and stamp their presence on the scene. Nonetheless, within punk circles, men and women could enjoy a certain level of equality that was distinct from that of mainstream society, as had also been the case for the hardcore scene in Tokyo (Milito Matsue 2009, 106).

Younger punks in Kyoto looked up to Ranko as a maternal figure. Twenty-nine years old when she first started playing music, she was older, and wiser, at least in her educational achievements. She had graduated from university with a degree in fashion and tried her hand at becoming a fashion designer; however, her designs did not sell well, as, she claimed, they were too eccentric (*Kyoto Daigaku Shinbun* 1 November 1988). Imai fondly remembered her as referring to him and his friends as *Shōnen GBH* (Young GBH; Seki et al. 2021). She booked bands, performed with her own successful groups (the Continental Kids and Sperma) and provided places for touring groups to stay while in Kansai. She was famous for outlandish stage performances, often wearing clothes that left little to the imagination or nothing at all. She gained coverage in men's magazines as a topless rocker who could titillate their non-punk readers with stories of her live performances (*Focus*, February 1988). For the mainly male journalists who wrote about her, Ranko, like Western female punks, gained acceptance in a sexist scene by flaunting her sexuality (Reddington 2012, 73). She recognized the power of her sexuality and was proud of it. Ranko was a significant player who had the respect of her peers; people listened to her opinions and went along with her policies (Ishibashi 2022).

In the mid-1980s, Beat Crazy began booking shows at Eggplant in Osaka while continuing to support young hardcore acts in Kyoto. Eggplant opened in 1984 in the working-class district of Nishinari in Osaka. K-Yan, the manager, was friends with Ranko, and she often went to stay with her in Kyoto. The two operated within similar networks and had shared experiences of groping and harassment at the hands of supposed fans. The Eggplant connection allowed the Kyoto scene to expand to Osaka; Sperma performed on Eggplant's opening night, and the venue became a mainstay for Beat Crazy events (*Kansai Hardcore* 2020, 91). Eggplant helped to transform the hardcore scene in Kansai. Bands could rehearse and book shows there quite easily. It had a big stage and no cut-off time, which was unusual for Osaka; in contrast, Kyoto already featured all-night Beat Crazy events. As Eggplant doubled as a rehearsal studio (and had a vending machine for beer), it became a central hang-out for local bands (Hopkins 2022), including the Osaka-based members of S.O.B. Tottsuan moved house to live close to it. Like the scene itself, Eggplant only lasted a few years, closing shortly after the Shōwa Emperor's death in 1989. Persistent complaints from locals about the noise forced the venue to shut its doors (*Kansai Hardcore* 2020, 95).

The two Kyoto-based members of S.O.B., Seki and Yasue, along with Imai attended Higashiyama Junior High School; Seki, who was a year ahead of Yasue and Imai, was the first among them to get into punk. In his third year of junior high (1982), he went to see the Clash in Osaka and often attended live shows by Japanese punks like Anarchy and Kyoto-based punks like the Continental Kids. Also, the first among them to start a band – the Bones – Seki became interested in hardcore punk. He was particularly intrigued by the violence associated with hardcore performances, having read about the Tokyo-based group G.I.S.M. (Seki 2021). While Seki himself did not feel that the Bones were overly violent, his band gained a reputation for violent performances and their fanbase populated by delinquents. Ta-Ko, who would go on to inherit Ranko's bar, Rose Garden, remembers marauding around Kyoto with other friends as the 'Bones Barmy Army', a direct appropriation of the football-hooligan culture associated with British skinhead oi punk (Ta-Ko 2021). The relatively small Kyoto hardcore scene interacted closely with other violent local scenes such as the skinheads (Imai, *El Zine* 57, 2022).

These young groups gathered around Beat Crazy events or at the all-age shows organized at Avix. Naoto was impressed by the Bones' aggressive live performances and immediately thought of bringing Seki into S.O.B. when its original guitar player quit. The Bones released one EP, *In A Sick Society!* on Noise Room Records in 1985. This record takes early British hardcore as its inspiration; the band had started out covering songs by Exploited, an influence reflected not only in the music but also in the mohawk hairstyles (*Zero Magazine 2* 2022, 29). Thanks to the patronage of Ranko and others in the Kyoto scene, the band also appeared on the 1986 compilation, *We Are Beat Crazy* (Captain Records), alongside the Continental Kids, Sperma, Cockney Cocks and Sekiri.

Like many others, Yasue was introduced to punk music through shared tapes of punk bands from junior high school classmates. However, he first discovered punk through Japanese acts such as Anarchy and the Tokyo Rockers, rather than through the more common route of listening to foreign bands like the Sex Pistols. Like most members of S.O.B. and young punks of his generation, the first live show he saw was the Stalin/Hijōkaidan show, organized by Beat Crazy at Seibu Kōdō in 1983. According to Jessica Schwartz, punk music is a rejection of rock music culture through musical techniques like extreme noise while also incorporating the visual cues from classic rock-and-roll (Schwartz 2015, 143); the Hijōkaidan/Stalin show demonstrated these characteristics. Like their US and UK counterparts, the Stalin also borrowed heavily from the rock-and-roll aesthetic but pushed the music to extremes, creating a seminal event for young punks in Kyoto. For Yasue, who had heard the band on the soundtrack to Ishii Gakuryū's cult movie *Burst City* the previous year, it was an impactful initiation to live music. Yause remembered the scene as being like a violent playground that he, in his youthful exuberance, found appealing. Going to events at Seibu Kōdō took him to another world; even after being chased out of the venue by the singer of the Bones, he was not deterred from going back to watch shows. Eventually he took part in them himself (Seki et al. 2021). One of Yasue's first bands, formed with Imai and other classmates, simply performed GBH covers. He and Imai then established the group Seltic Frost to perform covers and songs of their own.

Imai would later design the album cover art for *Don't Be Swindle*. Imai took a keen interest in art as a child and was

Figure 4 *Imai's alternative design for* Don't Be Swindle's *cover art was included as a sticker with the album and in poster art for the band's European tour (courtesy of S.O.B.).*

inspired by the manga artists of his day, copying pictures from comics he had amassed in his collection. Like many kids of his generation, he wished to become a manga artist. He was also influenced by his family home, where his grandfather ran an antique shop. Its large collection of traditional *suiboku* (monochrome ink) paintings depicting *yōkai* (monsters) also inspired his art, referencing the traditional aesthetics he'd inherited from his grandfather. His parents, fearing that he was spending too much time sketching and not enough time studying, one day threw out his manga collection. This was a turning point for Imai, who decided to drop out of school. Just as he was thinking of joining a motorcycle gang, punk rock came around.

Imai's first introduction to the genre was listening to the Sex Pistols. It was not the music but the design of the record sleeve that struck him the most. Imai's first time going to see a punk band live was also the aforementioned 1983 Stalin/Hijōkaidan show, which a friend's older sister suggested that they go see. His first impression of Seibu Kōdō was the exterior of the venue, which was covered in the debris of auto parts from the adjacent Kyoto University Mechanics' Club and other trash. As he recalled, the place looked like a Mad Max-style, post-apocalyptic landscape. During the show, the band, wearing gas masks and lab coats stained with fake blood, chained the exit doors and chased the audience around with shovels. The chaos and violence both shocked and impressed Imai. From then on, he and many others were converted to punk rock (Seki et al. 2021).

Impressed by what he had seen but having heard that hardcore bands were even more extreme, Imai began seeking out more shows in Kyoto, Osaka and Kobe. During his third year in junior high school, he started listening to UK hardcore acts such as Discharge, Chaos UK and Crass and began copying the artwork from the covers of their records, while also learning to play the guitar and bass. Around this time Imai also began designing and painting the backs of his friends' leather jackets. He was especially influenced by the styles of Pushead whose art heavily features skull motifs, such as on the Chaos UK 1982 EP *Loud, Political and Uncompromising* (Riot City Records). Pushead is perhaps more well known for his work with Metallica. He also did the artwork for the Japanese band Gastunk's *Under the Sun* (Pusmort 1987) (*El Zine* 2022). A key moment for Imai's development was when he met Pushead in Kyoto in 1986. Funnyara, the bass player from the Bones, had invited the artist to Japan (Imai 2015). Noticing that most bands in the area were not very good at creating an aesthetic, Imai intervened to design images to accompany information on upcoming shows. Again, access to his grandfather's antique shop also gave him access to high-quality paper, which was used in wrapping ceramics, and could be repurposed for his flyers (Seki et al. 2021).

As well as doing the art on the back of friends' leather jackets, painting skateboards and etching band logos onto butterfly knives, Imai also turned to designing and inking tattoos. He created a blueprint for a 'Kyoto City Tattoo Machine'. The very few tattoo parlours available, even if they could do the designs young Kyoto punks wanted, would not risk tattooing minors. Imai's art then quite literally got under the skin of the Kyoto punk scene (Imai 2015). Although Kyoto lacked places to practice, skateboarding suited Imai and others well. He found the cultural aspects of skateboarding appealing, the fashion, lifestyle and attitude connected to it and gleaned from flicking through skateboard magazines (Seki et al. 2021). Naoto had been also a keen skater before joining the band

and while others were getting their inspiration from record sleeves, Naoto was busy importing skateboard and fashion magazines. Reading through British magazines such as *i-D*, *Face* and especially *Thrasher* expanded his horizons. When he saw Rat Scabies (drummer for the Damned) wearing a *Thrasher* T-shirt in the 1983 documentary *UK/DK*, he was duly impressed and his interest in skating was given the punk seal of approval. Moving away from the customary leather jackets and boots into T-shirts and vans, the band stood out from the rest of the hardcore punk groups in Japan (*Zero Magazine 2* 2022, 20). Without leather jackets to advertise his artwork, Imai took to designing skateboards instead – a useful, portable billboard for one's work.

Don't Be Swindle was the second record cover that Imai designed for S.O.B., having done the artwork for their first EP, *Leave Me Alone* (1986). For *Don't Be Swindle*, Imai offered two designs; the second was adopted, with the first used as an accompanying sticker and a poster for the subsequent European tour. Despite not being in traditional manga style, the artwork honours Imai's obsession with Violent Jack, Go Nagai's well-known character who is referenced by the 'J' on the mask the character is holding. As a volatile, violent character whose signature weapon was a flick knife, Violent Jack fit right in with the band's ethos (Imai 2023). The character holding the mask is typical of the skull aesthetic that Imai had been developing since producing flyers for Seltic Frost. Appearing out of a pitch-black background, he points an accusatory finger at the viewer reinforcing the album's title. The back cover image and layout were designed by Naoto and it was he who approached Imai to do the cover art (*Zero Magazine* 2022, 82). Imai's cover art helped establish him as a 'punk' artist, although he considered it at the time as a simple throwaway; he certainly considered himself a punk, not an artist. The network of punks helped develop Imai's talent as well as providing spaces to display his work.

With her relentless energy, Ranko was instrumental in creating the music scene in Kyoto and wider Kansai. But as the 1990s got underway, she started to experience severe health problems. She fought uterine cancer for six years before, then 44, and passed away in November 1997. As Ishibashi Shōjirō wrote in his obituary for her in *Doll*, she was a formidable presence on stage and a wonderful person off it. She influenced all of the actors in the scene, big or small, in one way or another (*Doll* 126, February 1998). She and the other Beat Crazy members built the infrastructure that nourished the nascent hardcore scene. Kyoto is a relatively small city, so the hardcore scene had to coexist with other genres in shared spaces. Perhaps being subsumed under the Beat Crazy all-genre umbrella gave the young punks to reconsider their attitudes towards violence. According to Nakamura Shintarō, punks were less into the violence by the late 1980s and shied away from getting involved in mid-show fights. He thought that a more respectful relationship at shows developed between audience, performers and staff, who were usually in bands themselves (Nakamura 2022).

It's important to remember that a passion for music and live performances drove the formation of this habitus and the scene that followed. Indeed, without the music, the scene could not have been sustained. Kyoto was the recognized centre of extreme noise, and S.O.B.'s performances reflect this legacy. When comparing two S.O.B. live shows from 1986 at Seibu Kōdō – one featuring the original lineup and the other featuring Seki and Yasue – we can hear a noticeable increase in the band's intensity, even if the audio quality is different.

The two versions of the upcoming *Don't Be Swindle* track, 'I'm a Dreamer', are where this difference is most apparent. Kyoto bands were afforded the chance to develop their extreme sound because Seibu Kōdō was such a large venue. Yasue was concerned about producing extreme hardcore music for a more diverse audience while simultaneously minimizing audience violence. This was particularly true at hardcore shows, where the gender disparity would diminish slightly as the band's popularity grew following the release of *Don't Be Swindle* (Seki et al. 2021).

4 *Don't Be Swindle*

Squeezing in eighteen tracks in a mere 20 minutes, 35 seconds, *Don't Be Swindle* is a statement of the band's speed and intensity. As David Kato Hopkins notes, S.O.B. sounds 'like no one else. It's as if they had heard descriptions of the crazy and wild music called hardcore and without ever having heard a hardcore band, decided to make their own' (Hopkins 2015, 203). The album's breakneck tempo connected to other extremes in the Kansai music scene, such as the noise of Hijōkaidan or the radical lyrics of the 1960s folk generation; extremes became a common link among Kyoto's various scenes over time. While S.O.B. was primarily a live band, *Don't Be Swindle* became its sonic showcase. Here we turn our attention to the album's composition.

Before *Don't Be Swindle*, S.O.B. had released their first EP, *Leave Me Alone* (Selfish Records 1986), and had appeared on the compilation, *Last Punk Osaka* (Beggars Connection 1986). Seki and Yasue joined the band for the recording, but only after the tracks for *Leave Me Alone* were written. However, their guitar and drum styles added a sense of urgency to the band's musical style (*Zero Magazine 2* 2022, 33). Both Yasue and Seki were influenced not only by UK hardcore but also American thrash metal, particularly S.O.D. and their guitar and drumming style, which Yasue claims to be the first style of blast beat. (It is merely a coincidence that S.O.B. and S.O.D. shared similar acronyms, at least according to Yasue.) *Leave Me Alone* was released about six months before Napalm Death's influential album *Scum* (Earache Records, 1987). Highlighting the

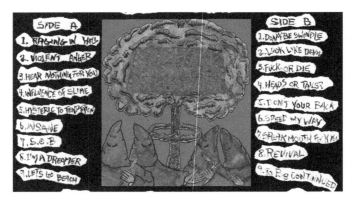

Figure 5 *Detail from the back cover showing the track listing and Naoto's apocalyptic artwork (courtesy of S.O.B.).*

importance of the tape-sharing community in hardcore punk circles, Napalm Death listed S.O.B. in the thanks/inspiration section of the liner notes to *Scum*.

Having only joined the band for touring and the recording sessions of *Leave Me Alone*, *Don't Be Swindle* was Seki's first chance to write songs for the band and fully shape their grindcore sound. Like most of their contemporaries, S.O.B. were primarily a live band, and the goal of the recording was to capture the live sound as accurately as possible (*Fool's Mate* 75, 1987, 25). Tottsuan hoped the record, with its rough and ready recording, would reflect the intensity of attending a live performance, although without the physical contact necessary to enhance the experience. The songs were recorded at Gorilla Studio in Osaka, with the band recording the drums, bass and guitar parts all together, a recording process they would use in later records (*Doll* 195, 2003, 83). Some classify S.O.B.'s musical style as fastcore, which features fast tempos and brief songs (Namekawa 2007, 82). However, it is more often described as blast beat or grindcore. Although blast beat and grindcore are sometimes used interchangeably, blast beat generally refers to the drum sound, while grindcore refers to the genre. Discharge's 1982 album *Hear Nothing, Say Nothing* (Clay Records) is arguably the first recorded example of the style. By the mid-1980s, several punk-metal crossover bands began to make blast beat 'the rhythmic foundation of entire songs or sections of songs', with the label grindcore applied to groups that adopted this approach (Pearson 2021, 105). It is best personified by Napalm Death drummer Mick Harris, although he makes no claims to be its originator, it would define his band's sound.

Blast beat also dominates *Don't Be Swindle*. David Pearson, one of the few scholars to look at grindcore/blast beat from a musicological perspective, describes two main approaches to the blast beat. The first, which he calls the alternating kick and snare blast beat (AKS), beats these two drums in rapid alternation, usually with a hi-hat or ride cymbal played in tandem with the kick drum. As Pearson explains, this is a hardcore beat, but the 'pulse is completely filled with kick and snare drum, and the alternation between the two is sped up to the limits of what is physically possible' (Pearson 2021, 105–6). The second approach, the simultaneous kick and snare blast beat (SKS), strikes the kick and snare drum at the same time, along with a cymbal. This creates 'a continuous pulse stream with all the drums sounding simultaneously rather than alternating' (Pearson 2021, 106). While the latter approach is slower than the first, both methods create a sense of extreme speed. Finally, Pearson highlights the value placed on the visual performance of blast-beat drumming. Drummers make a display of the physical effort required to drum at such speed, so that the audience can both see and hear the strain involved in the performance (Pearson 2021, 107).

Listening to proto-hardcore of SS alongside S.O.B., one hears how grindcore evolved from using more crash cymbal instead of hi-hat to create the pulse.[1] Mick Harris described blast beat as simply a hardcore beat – kick-snare-kick-snare with an alternation between the ride and crash cymbals (Harris 2022). Yasue explained that his style is based on a jazz beat, with fill patterns simply being replaced with the main beat, all the while being sped up. Blast beat was a style Yasue had been experimenting with while in Seltic Frost, but S.O.B. gave him a chance to realize it (Seki et al. 2021). In grindcore and metal, blast-beat drumming is distinguished through performance. Grindcore drummers prefer not to use a double-bass-drum pedal, as it would lessen the physical effort required to play and thus diminish the spectacle. Pearson notes that during the 1990s, extreme hardcore drumming could clock up speeds of 400 BPM. The drumming on *Don't Be Swindle* does not quite reach these limits, but the feeling of speed is present. Rather than sensing a distinct pulse, blast beat creates a 'whirlwind of abrasive accents' from the rapid strikes of the kick, snare and cymbal (Pearson 2019, 11). *Don't Be Swindle*'s first track, 'Raging in Hell', gives us an example of this whirlwind and sets the tone for the rest of the album. It begins with around twenty seconds of heavy bass and guitar riffs set to a standard rock beat of about 120 BPM, then accelerates to a peak of blast-beat madness at around 250 BPM, to average around 175 BPM.[2] Considering the kick drum, snare and cymbals, Yasue averages at 700 strikes per minute. We can also note from this track, and generally throughout

---

[1]   SS *The Original 12"* (released on Alchemy in 1984 but recorded in 1979).

[2]   Thanks to Jacob Dunlap of the Kyoto band Black Hours for calculating BPM.

the album, that Yasue favours the alternating kick and snare (AKS) approach, although the track 'Fuck or Die' is more akin to simultaneous kick and snare (SKS).

Matching the intensity of the music, the lyrics to 'Raging in Hell' conjure up violent images of cannibalism and beatings. Mixed English and Japanese lyrics are also heard repeatedly throughout the album, making the band's message clear to English speaking listeners, despite many grammatical errors. Even without seeing them live, we can tell what kind of band we're dealing with from the first song, which exhorts us to 'lose reason' and 'Be Violent Crazy'. The following track, 'Violent Anger', continues the theme by calling out pretentious liars. Beginning with a heavy bass riff, the track features the band's style of call-and-response lyrics. Like 'Raging in Hell', it also alternates between slower and blast beats, demonstrating the band's ability to play conventional punk rock.

The blast beat is perhaps at its most intense and sustained on the track, 'Don't Your Back', where Tottsuan screams over a persistent 200 BPM, 'No regrets, don't think about the past' (kōkai suruna, kako no koto wa kangaezu). A key aim of blast beat is to play as fast as possible; S.O.B., which has earned recognition as the fastest band in Japan, aspired to be the fastest band in the world (Ishiya 2020b, 53). Playing at this speed requires not only physical endurance but also technical mastery. Indeed, the songs' extreme speed, brevity and sudden tempo changes necessitate expert timing and coordination among the musicians. As Pearson points out, this need challenges the preconception that punk does not concern itself with technical prowess and can be played by mere amateurs (Pearson 2021, 107). The track 'Hysteric to Temptation' gives us an indication of this skill. It begins with Yasue's blast beat but suddenly jumps into a bass groove layered with Seki's guitar riffs before transitioning back into the blast beat. These transitions are evident on the longer tracks on the album, with the band seamlessly moving from blast beat to slower grooves. Not only do the changes in tempo help to highlight technical ability, but they also afford Yasue a break and highlights the faster speed when the tempo does increase. 'Hysteric to Temptation' also illuminates the live sound and S.O.B.'s connections to oi punk and early hardcore. As the bass groove cuts in, Tottsuan and the band do a simple call-and-response on 'oi'. During live shows, the audience would participate, which marked the band from its contemporaries. For example, Napalm Death's *Scum* is a more confrontational album, with no call-and-response anthems.

Grindcore fans also prefer short tracks, where a band can instantly start and stop in unison to highlight how tight a unit they are. An example of such a track is 'SxOxB', which has a quick burst of blast beat. At just over two seconds, it is one of the shortest punk songs of all time, although not quite as short as Napalm Death's one-second 'You Suffer'. A brief thud of drums, bass and guitar allows the band to scream its name before the song ends. A favourite of live audiences, it often closes out the show. Subsequent tracks, such as 'Speak Mouth Fuck You', similarly has short, sharp bursts just long enough to yell the track's title and also displays the band's tight-knit performance. While Yasue's drumming is at the heart of the band's sound, Seki's guitar riffs form the foundation for song composition. They fit the grindcore style: down-tuned guitars, heavy distortion and downstrokes or tremolo picking to play one note repeatedly. This is bolstered by Naoto's overdriven bass. Seki was greatly influenced by his brother, who played drums in a heavy metal band and taught Yasue. Seki's guitar keeps pace with the blast beat with impressive riffs (such as on 'Insane'), and he occasionally squeezes in a solo ('Look like Devil'). To shift power chords rapidly in fast tempo, he began to play a heavy-metal style guitar, the Fernandes Rhoads (although Randy Rhoads may not have approved of Seki's technique).[3] (Seki now uses an ESP; the company even released a guitar model with his signature.) Seki also began the process of composing songs by developing a riff, with the rest of the band building a structure around it. In line with the band's philosophy, he claimed that the songwriting process was a collaborative effort. While everyone wrote specific sections, they all checked each other's work and offered advice as they went along (*Fool's Mate* 75 1987, 25).

Hardcore punk is often sung deliberately in a way that makes it nearly impossible to understand the lyrics. According to Greg Bennick of the band Trial, singing in hardcore 'sounds like "unholy hell" to the layperson, and the truth is, they sound like unholy hell to all of us' (Ambrosch 2018, 8). Napalm Death vocalist Lee Dorrian explained why he sang with such urgency in an interview for the BBC British children's TV show, *What's That Noise*, in 1989. While performing, the lyrics raced through his mind, and he had to keep up with the volume, speed and intensity of the music, making pronouncing the lyrics difficult (BBC 1989). As Gerfried Ambrosch demonstrates, the 'inarticulacy' is not incidental, but rather, an essential part of punk's aesthetic of dissent, and it is meaningful on its own (Ambrosch 2018, 12). Tottsuan's process of writing lyrics also fits this mode. He added the lyrics only after the tracks were completed: for him, it was critical for the vocals to fit the sound; eloquence was not a priority (*Fool's Mate* 75,

---

[3] The Fernandes Rhoads is a Japanese-produced copy of Jackson's Randy Rhoads signature guitar.

1987, 25). Tottsuan gave his vocals an antagonistic and abrasive tone, sounding emotive and selfish. As a result, his vocals are frequently indecipherable, whether in Japanese or English, and to fully understand the message, the listener must become a reader (Ambrosch 2018, 17). As with most hardcore releases, the album includes a lyric sheet. The album's themes include personal issues, politics and simple entertainment. Despite the challenging aural aesthetic, hardcore lyrics serve as a basis for dialogue between the singer and the listener/reader.

Indeed, the priority for the vocalist was to match the many riffs and beats crammed into one track. Tottsuan's vocals match the speed of the blast beat, so that the lyrics are coherent only when the beat slows down to an appropriate pace. One might question whether lyrics are necessary when they are so difficult to hear. However, punk lyrics are important in that they give the scene its collective 'poetic voice' (Ambrosch 2018, 12). Yasue believed that the lyrics prompted S.O.B. members to think about the messages or slogans that they wanted to convey to their audience (Seki et al. 2021).

As Bennick respectfully notes, hardcore lyrics may be direct and confrontational because the bands lack the ability to write lyrics. It is also the case that punk rock lyrics are active, not passive. Hardcore punk is a participatory experience; the music, lyrics and live performance demand a reaction from the audience (Ambrosch 2018, 9). S.O.B.'s lyrics became more complex as their sound developed in subsequent albums. After touring Europe, they began writing more in English, although not exclusively. While the prose on *Don't Be Swindle* is not eloquent, they offer an insight into the mindset of Kansai's young punks. The three tracks 'Influence of Slime', 'Hysteric to Temptation' and 'Insane', for example, reflect on mental health. Tottsuan was suffering from a lot of frustration while preparing for the album, and writing lyrics helped to express his state of mind (*Fool's Mate* 75 1987, 25). For him, singing about exploding skulls ('Influence of Slime'), giving into temptations ('Hysteric to Temptation') and the fear of losing control ('Insane') was a cathartic release of this stress.

Further commentary on punks' social lives can be found in the track 'Speed My Way', a double entendre on drugs and S.O.B.'s sound and playing style, with Tottsuan claiming the band members are 'only speed freak [*sic*]'. Much writing about Japanese music scenes denies or minimizes the use of illicit substances by scene members. Drug use was not uncommon, but those who want to discuss it openly are few and far between. Most all-age shows did not serve alcohol because most of the audience was under the legal drinking age (which is twenty in Japan); instead, many people turned to alternatives like paint thinner, which is widely available in arts and crafts stores, for a short, sharp buzz. Many people would later upgrade (or downgrade) to methamphetamine, also known as shabu. Other tracks such as 'Heads or Tails' offer a more positive message, as Tottsuan frantically lays the lyrics, 'live or die, take a chance, that's all you have' (ikiru ka shinu ka ichi kaba chika yatte miro omae ni wa sore shika nai), onto the beat. Its live performances were built on audience participation, with the call-and-response of 'heads or tails' forming the chorus.

Hardcore punk in Japan shared its nihilistic rejection of the status quo with its UK counterpart but did not otherwise fully import the politics (Hopkins 2015, 177–9). The two tracks that end side one highlight a more innocent form of rebellion. 'I'm a Dreamer' is almost a pop song; at least the opening riff leads you to believe so. It reminds us of Naoto's skills as a bass player (as his bass line leads the track) and demonstrates Seki's ability to write a catchy riff when he wants to. The lyrics, written in a mix of Japanese and English, focus on punk's simple DIY and egotistical ethos, stating, 'I'm only moving towards one goal' (Ore wa hitotsu no yume ni mukatte susumu dake): 'Dream my way, my thinking, my living, my carry on'. 'Let's Go Beach' is the album's longest track, lasting 1 minute and 54 seconds, nearly breaking the two-minute mark! Naoto's bass lines lead the track, which resembles a Shonen Knife song more than a hardcore punk number. A participatory song in performance, it conjures up the rather comical image of Tottsuan exhorting fans to do a backstroke in the mosh pit while he leads the audience in a chorus of 'Let's go summer beach!' Many bands, including Brutal Truth (1997), have covered this song, perhaps because it has clear vocals in English, a great hook and a fun vibe. Hardcore punk, with its connection to urban environments, seems out of place for relaxing on the beach, as in these lyrics. However, it makes for an entertaining end to side one, providing some respite before the heavier content on side two.

Two other songs exclusively in English are 'Revival' and 'To Be Continued'. 'Revival' is a tribute to youth and the combination of violence, purity and power it can provide. In its jumbled syntax, 'Youth of Power' (rather than 'Power of Youth') forwards an interesting image of young people as the wellspring of power. Most Japanese hardcore bands wrote English lyrics frequently, and S.O.B. were not afraid to write the majority of their lyrics in English, despite their limited abilities and grammatical mistakes. According to Hopkins, hardcore bands and other rebellious youth in Japan used foreign means to express their stance. To be truly punk meant rejecting some aspects of one's Japanese identity, and singing in English was one way of doing so (Hopkins 2015, 177). Using English also connected the band with a wider audience. After touring

Europe, S.O.B. used English even more frequently in lyrics and stage announcements.

The title track, 'Don't Be Swindle', opens side two of the album. Content-wise, it's a typical punk song, and given that Imai cites the Sex Pistols as an influence, the title seems likely inspired by that English band's 'Great Rock'n'Roll Swindle'. The lyrics, a mix of Japanese and English, enter after the opening bass riff, declaring, 'They're all full of crap' (*kudaranai mono bakaride*), and 'you're going to get fooled' (*Damasaren no wa omae da*). The tempo slows down for the singalong chorus which is a simple repeat of 'don't be swindle'. In correct grammar, the title would be 'Don't Be Swindled', as the song demands that we open our eyes and avoid being duped. Indeed, the band would later correct themselves in the lyrics of 'Public Eye' from the 1994 album *Vicious World*, where they cry, 'Don't Be Swindled'. The theme continues to the next track, 'Look like Devil', which declares, 'They've taken all I had, drained my blood, left me like a corpse' (Ore no subete o ubaitori, ketsueki made mo sui torare, shitai no yō ni natte). They express their anger at exploitation most bluntly when they shout, 'Fuck you, hurry up, get out', in 'Fuck or Die', in the clearest English pronunciation on the album. While the lyrics may be generic, Tottsuan's delivery, in tandem with the music's frantic pace, mould them into a much more menacing expression.

The album concludes with a question: 'To Be Continued?' It's a repetitive drum loop with the band asking the question, then screaming and laughing into the fadeout. Here and elsewhere on the record, notably 'Let's Go Beach', we see a playful side of hardcore, a genre that is often stereotyped as overly morbid or serious. At a New Year's Eve gig at Eggplant, the band promised attendees a secret gift. Fans who expected a flexidisc or other merchandise may have been disappointed to receive only an orange. Unsurprisingly, the stage and streets surrounding Eggplant were plastered with the fruit (Hopkins 2022). Although not as visceral as being pelted with raw meat as at Hijōkaidan shows, the band parodied the Kansai punk tradition of creating a mess for the owners to clean up.

After *Don't Be Swindle*, S.O.B. released four more full-length studio albums, including *What's the Truth?* (1990), *Gate of Doom* (1993), *Vicious World* (1994) and *Dub Grind* (1999). They would also return to their back catalogue in 2003 with an album of covers of their own songs, *Still Grind Attitude*, which allowed new vocalist Etsushi to stretch his lungs. *What's the Truth?* found the band's sound going in a more metal direction; it crossed the thin line between hardcore punk and thrash metal, which both use blast-beat-style drumming. According to Pearson, punk conventions emerged from shared interests among multiple bands, and a smaller group of bands later crystallized these conventions as part of new standards (Pearson 2021, 10). S.O.B. helped to establish a new standard for hardcore punk, and the album solidified their claim to elite status. The release of an album also increased touring opportunities, allowing the band's sound to spread beyond Kansai and Japan.

5 Heads or tails? The live scene after *Don't Be Swindle*

The release of *Don't Be Swindle* marked S.O.B. as the representative of a second generation of hardcore, with the music press naming them as the vanguard of a hardcore renaissance (*Fool's Mate* 75 1987, 24). The first generation of hardcore bands – Gauze, Lip Cream, Outo and Seki's previous band, the Bones – had formed a relatively large scene. In an indication of how quickly music scenes ebb and flow, the music magazine *Rock File* noted in 1988 that a hardcore revival was already forming, referring to it as 'strong style' (words borrowed from professional wrestling; *Rock File* 1988, 30). This revival was in essence a marketing gimmick connected to the band boom of the late 1980s and early 1990s, which reinvigorated the live music scene in Japan.

This chapter focuses on S.O.B. and the live scene in Kansai in 1988–9. The approach of a new decade saw not only growth in new music but also the worsening health of the Showa emperor, which brought politics back to centre stage of the music scene. Politics was a thorny question for the new punk scene: on one hand, it rejected the politicized messaging of the old left; on the other hand, it benefitted from the same spaces and artistic infrastructure, which had afforded the wild shows that were the hallmark of the scene. S.O.B. was never overtly political, nor was most of the scene. But in 1989, to be different and defiant in Japan, and proud and loud about it, was instantly political. The energy and defiance of hardcore performance had new meaning in the political context of late-1980s Japan.

In her highly acclaimed account of the reckoning with the Showa era in 1989, Norma Field mentions in passing that punk rockers were one of few groups that dared to challenge the hypocrisy and amnesia of mainstream media and society regarding the emperor's wartime role: 'Punk rock musicians sport[ed] banners opposing the emperor system [and] were routinely roughed up by the National Security Police' (Field 1993, 188). While Field does not elaborate further, the connections between punk and politics at the time were significant. As Oguma Eiji and Mōri Yoshitaka have posited, punks in Japan were important in the anti-nuclear movement in the 1980s, and they were early joiners of movements that countered the tide of triumphant neoliberalism that took over Japan during the bubble years (Mōri 2009, 120; Oguma 2022). Unlike Western bands like Crass and Conflict and some punks in Tokyo, however, S.O.B. and most Kansai punks were not directly political. They rarely showed any interest or displayed any political motivation in the conventional sense. This does not mean they were apolitical.

1989 provided an opportunity for the Kyoto scene to display its connection to a longer history of resistance at Seibu Kōdō. The death of the Showa emperor brought a sombre atmosphere as Japanese citizens were expected to pay respect to the emperor. Punks were at the forefront of opposing the enforced silence. They were particularly suited to leading this role as what punks saw as their right to make noise was in stark contrast with the silence around them. And Kyoto punks were renowned for noise. The punk habitus that grew out of

Seibu Kōdō was all about noise and defiance. As Mōri argued, Kyoto punks had no specific message: 'they were just defying established norms. Machida from Inu, Hijōkaidan and [others] were urinating on stage, etc., [but] had no idea what they were doing. Even so, they were clearly defying something' (Mōri 2009, 122). There was no message or structure to S.O.B. and others' defiance, but with Hirohito's death and the silence that followed, punks became political, even if they didn't express it that way.

The politics of punk were only part of a bigger problem for S.O.B. The industry was unable to fit them into a single box. The issue of categorizing the band was the focus of the music media, not the band members themselves. Was it a skate-rock band or a new generation of hardcore? What were their politics? When listening to the track 'Hear Nothing for You' on *Don't Be Swindle*, we might hear a political statement in the lyrics, '[You] come in on the right and go out on the left' (migi kara haitte hidari e nukeru). However, we might also be reading too much into that lyric to claim it as a political song: it may also simply mean that someone's words are going in one ear and out of the other. When asked about the band's opinions on current social issues or politics, Tottsuan replied, he would be lying if he said he had no interest in politics, but also, as a band, they could not exert that much influence. He saw political decisions as foisted on society from higher-ups and enforced by the police. He preferred to avoid politics and sing about more everyday frustrations (*Fool's Mate* 75 1987, 25).

As a live band first and foremost, S.O.B. collaborated with bands or performed at events that had more explicit political connections than they themselves claimed. One of their first live shows after the release of *Don't Be Swindle* was with Hijōkaidan under the combined name, S.O.B. Kaidan. Tottsuan had approached Hijōkaidan, saying that the Sta-Kaidan show at Seibu Kōdō had heavily influenced him and that he hoped the two bands could perform together (Hiroshige 2013, 74). The S.O.B. Kaidan line-up consisted of elder statesmen from the Kansai noise scene – Jojo Hiroshige and Hayashi Naoto, along with S.O.B. and Yamatsuka Eye (Boredoms and Hanatarash). They covered tracks from *Don't Be Swindle*: 'Fuck or Die', 'Raging in Hell', 'Look like Devil' and 'To Be Continued'. While most of the tracks maintained the brief intensity of the original recordings, 'To Be Continued' was stretched out to a ten-minute feedback drone, with the same stop-start drum beat looping repeatedly.

They had initially planned to play a show at La Mama in Shibuya, Tokyo. However, due to excessive violence and damage to the venue, the group was left with a hefty bill and potential legal action. As the members of S.O.B. were minors, the organizer and owner of Alchemy Records, Hayashi Naoto, was held liable. An extra performance at Eggplant was thus arranged and released as a VHS titled *Noise, Violence and Destroy* through Alchemy Records, with proceeds going towards paying off the owners of La Mama (Hiroshige 2013, 80).[1] The event sparked the hasty birth of the label's video division. The Osaka show was wilder than the one in Tokyo; the band had the backing of Eggplant's owners to go as crazy as they liked. With Yasue throwing drum cymbals from behind him like frisbees, Hiroshige wondered how the audience managed to escape without serious injury (Hiroshige 2013, 82). S.O.B. thus joined a long list of collaborators with Jojo Hiroshige, engaging in controversy and destruction while further cementing the connections between the Japanese noise and punk scenes.

---

[1]   Remastered and reissued in 2022.

The standout event in Kyoto in the late 1980s was the three-day event, Cry Day, in January 1989. Just as Seibu Kōdō began the 1980s with a controversial event – The Police incident – it ended the decade with another controversy, this time involving S.O.B. Cry Day was organized to mark the passing of the Shōwa emperor, defying the enforcement of silence in Japanese public spaces during a period of national mourning. While they did not organize the event, S.O.B. performed alongside most Kyoto's punk bands at the time. Cry Day may not have been a watershed moment in S.O.B.'s career, but like the Police concert, it exemplified the contours of the scene in which the band operated, influencing their outlook and music. As Dunn explained, 'With punk, the message is the medium, and the medium is the message' (Dunn 2016, 157). This event demonstrated that messages did at times become political. Unlike earlier generations of bands, S.O.B. shied away from overt political messages; nonetheless, the dividing line between overt and covert politics in punk, and in Kyoto itself, between the student activists and the mostly working-class punks, did not always hold and tended to blur on occasion.

Much of this development can be explained by the punk habitus that grew out of the Seibu Kōdō scene, which was quite like the politicized scenes examined by Alan O'Connor in North America (O'Connor 2002, 227). The similarities between American and Japanese scenes were not accidental. Scenes, as examined in earlier chapters, are the result of connections to multiple such habitus and influences. The Kyoto scene depended on physical locations and people. Its commitment to counter cultural spaces came out of a very localized history, but it was also connected to larger global networks, where politics, especially in the West of the 1980s, was an important factor. Political lyrics, anti-war slogans on T-shirts and albums, and general anarchist discourse were part and parcel of punk culture, even if it meant very little for most Japanese punks (many denizens of the scene were high school dropouts and were not particularly strong in English). Like San Francisco punks who 'were identified by their obligatory Crass apparel' (Patton 2018, 138), Kyoto punks looked to London and were inspired by their 'Stop the City' actions. They identified with the UK punks' anger and defiance rather than the political agenda per se. Thus, it was only 'natural' for bands like S.O.B. to insert their own general sense of defiance into a more structured anti-imperialist action that their peers in Seibu Kōdō offered them. The older activists and politically informed students around Seibu Kōdō provided the organization and historical precedence for these actions, but the punks fit right in.

It was the silence forced on Japanese society in 1988–9 that politicized S.O.B.'s general delinquency and defiance. From Emperor Hirohito's collapse in September 1988 to his death in January 1989 and funeral several weeks later, Japan experienced two contradictory phenomena. For the first time in more than a generation, society attempted to reflect seriously on Japan as an aggressor in the Asia-Pacific War and the emperor's role in it. At the same time, as Norma Field noted, 'such newly critical reflection was truncated or repressed altogether by a spectacular exercise in self-censorship' (Field 1993, XV). The state, mainstream society and especially the media went to extraordinary lengths to ensure the 'proper' atmosphere. The Ministry of Education, for instance, sent notices to the prefectures that directed principals 'to take measures ensuring that their pupils understood the meaning of mourning and especially urging the observance of silent prayer' (Field 1993, 187). Following the emperor's passing, television stations removed all commercials and dedicated the next few days to programming that reflected on the emperor. For a month afterwards, entertainment, including performing arts and music, was excluded from programming, while stores eliminated such sounds over speakers as ambient music, announcements of discount sales and speeches (Abe 2018, 174). From the time the emperor had fallen ill in fall 1988, local festivals, annual music awards, fashion shows, kabuki theatre and countless other events were cancelled, and silence fell on the nation. *Jishuku* (self-restraint) was the order of the day. Abe Marié describes *jishuku* as 'a complex process and mechanism of social management, requiring an ensemble of institutions from mass media, local and national government, the police, right wing and private organizations, which create[d] the conditions of the majority of citizens to participate in self-silencing' (Abe 2018, 176). Her work highlights the long-term impact of this enforced silence on street performers in Tokyo.

To all this, the Kyoto punks said a hearty 'fuck you'. The Cry Day (or X-Day) events were intended to break the restraints of respectable society through the vehicles of radical art and loud music. The event was planned by student radicals and others connected to the Seirenkyō and related organizations. In December 1987, with the emperor's health already in significant decline, they convened at Seibu Kōdō for the 'first day of exchange and thinking about X-Day' (Daiichikai X dē o kangaeru kōryū shūkai); X-Day was the day designated by the media as the day of the emperor's passing. In the meeting, Ikeda Hiroshi, a professor of German literature and long-time activist with the student movement, told participants, 'We are now in Seibu Kōdō, which is a base of [free] expression, surrounded by the established order. We must say NO! (English in the original) to the effort by the enemy side to use X-Day as a tool to attack us and fortify the emperor system.' Emphasizing the unique character of autonomy at the site, Ikeda continued, 'We must make the best use of Seibu Kōdō and its freedom ... to promote that end' (*Kyoto Daigaku Shinbun* 1 January 1989). For Ikeda and his colleagues, breaking the silence around the emperor's wartime role was a direct continuation of their actions since the 1960s. Students and associated radicals led the movement to commemorate X-Day with a day of resistance, and it is not clear to what extent the punk scene participated in planning the event.

As the more-than-forty bands slated to perform on X-Day have attested, there were abundant connections between the political and artistic/musical scenes around the site. Both groups shared the space and a similar understanding of Seibu Kōdō as a site of autonomy and a 'base for freedom of expression'. According to Ishibashi Shōjirō, if you wanted to perform, 'the *Seirenkyō* would check your political beliefs,

Figure 6 *A different impression of Seibu kōdō, as it hosts debates during the X-Day event (courtesy of Kyoto University Newspaper Photo Archives* 京都大学新聞写真アーカイブ).

so as long as you passed the check, you were all right' and can do whatever you wanted. But, Ishibashi added casually, 'of course we were all left wing' (Ishibashi 2022). Neither Ishibashi nor S.O.B. members seemed to have given so much thought to politics, not then or now. They were left-wing by default and committed to maintaining the autonomy of the dorms and the hall, but their involvement was minimal. Wada Ryōichi, a founding Beat Crazy member and a Kyoto University student, was more educated and involved than hardcore scene members. However, his band Vampire did not perform, as he had just graduated from university and started working (Wada 2022). Other Beat Crazy regulars did play and identified with the goals of the X-Day movement. What became the Cry Day festival was a celebration of everything the place stood for, and the punk movement was an integral part of it. For Yasue, 'the business with the Showa emperor was a definitive event' in his personal history, as the character of the Seibu Kōdō scene really showed itself (Seki et al. 2021). Imai and others were equally impressed and had vivid memories from Cry Day (Kanda et al. 2021).

Seibu Kōdō was central to Cry Day as both a site and a habitus. Activists emphasized the long history of resistance to the imperial system in Kyoto radical circles. On the second reflection day in February 1988, Saitō Raitarō, then eighty-five, gave a lecture to participants. Saitō had been arrested in 1937 for his anti-imperialist activities. A long-time theatre critic, actor and director, Saito ran an anti-fascist movement, which operated in Kyoto's jazz *kissa* and theatres before the Second World War and was long associated with left-wing politics and avant-garde culture. During the next day's meetings, other political and cultural figures who were long involved in Seibu Kōdō, like the Wind Troupe's (*Kaze no ryodan*) Sakurai Daizō, also gave lectures on the history of the student and culture movement based around the site. Activists reached out to other groups, discussed the creation of circulars and attempted to reach out to a broader audience. The connections between culture, especially music, and politics were a frequent topic in the meetings. In the meeting on 24 April, an activist named Hirai (no first name given), spoke about the need to reach out to a wider public 'who is attached to the imperial family through the media' and create momentum to entice them away from corporate power structures through the power of culture. Hirai urged the movement to find a 'middle ground just like, for example, the jazz *kissa* was in the past' that could serve this purpose and attract 'the youth, the old, and the like' (*Kyoto Daigaku Shinbun* 1 January 1989).

Cry Day itself was intended not as a welcoming middle ground but as a celebration of extremes and defiance in all its forms. On 8 January, a barricade of discarded furniture, tires and cars was erected near Seibu Kōdō. Yasue vividly remembered the sense of danger and how the barrier reinforced the feeling of separation between the site and the outside world: 'a lot of [right-winger] trucks came down the road and seemed to be coming [our] way. I think there were about eight trucks … We thought to ourselves, "This is bad; something extreme is about to happen." Outside, right-wingers were screaming, but the left wing [inside] was not buying it' (Seki et al. 2021). Imai and Yasue were particularly impressed by a theatre production in which a figure representing the emperor was hanged, his head severed and displayed on a *yagura* (tower used as floats in traditional festivals). The play was probably 'The Sorrow of Yaponezia' (*Waga kanashimi no yaponezia*), which was performed by *Kaze no ryodan* and featured the burning of the Japanese flag. 'A music gig was held inside, while a theater troupe performed the suicide of the Shōwa emperor outside. That's Seibu Kōdō [for you].' Yasue recalled, 'If I were a right-winger, I would also be angry at seeing a scene where the emperor's head was hanged … The barricade created a boundary, and it was amazing.' The day had 'become definitive for me with the emperor Showa [event]' (Seki et al. 2021). Though Imai felt the meaning of the event was unclear, he cryptically acknowledged that 'ideologically, there is always a comparative idea of what it means' (Seki et al. 2021).

Similar ambivalence was displayed in Tokyo in an event that took place a week later, on 15 January with bands like Wakampu Junkies, Hellnation (on tour from the United States), Theze, and others. *MRR* reported that the event featured both hardcore bands and 'some serious leftist bands that set up a banner that said simply "sayonara Hirohito" and were passing out leaflets stating their opposition to the emperor system'. According to the anonymous reporter, his band and another hardcore band had 'a simple "fuck war, lets party"-type attitude'. The reporter was ambivalent about the radicals' serious politics (*MRR* 71, April 1989). Nonetheless, the report, like many reports and literature on Cry Day, provided a nuanced understanding (if somewhat problematic at times) of Hirohito's wartime role and Japan's crimes in Asia, mentioning the comfort-women issue, the Nanking massacre and other atrocities. Still, he concluded, 'perhaps there is some truth to what the leftists in Japan say about the dead emperor. He's dead though, and I really can't see so much hard evidence against the dude' (*MRR* 71, April 1989). Such divergence of opinions would not have been welcome inside the barricade at Seibu Kōdō, and it is easy to see why some S.O.B. members, and the *MRR* reporters were somewhat uneasy with the conformity and seriousness displayed by the activists. But flag burning and hanging emperors were radical acts that they could comprehend and admire.

S.O.B., along with forty other punk and hardcore bands, were drawn to Cry Day by its energy and defiance, not by any specific political message. What mattered was the boundary between their world of free expression, fuck-you attitude, and pure speed and noise, *vs.* the silence outside. At noon on 8 January, the organizing committee delivered a short speech that captured the event's us-vs.-them atmosphere. After describing the 'pathetic state of Japan' in which the media sang the deceased emperor's praises, the committee declared, 'We have been creating our own "sound" for many years at Seibu Kōdō, and I believe that X-Day is the time to put [our music] to the test. During the nationwide self-restraint in song, dance, and music, I am glad to know that Seibu Kōdō is doing something like this' (*Kyōto Daigaku Shinbun* 1 January 1989).

Following the speech, the Seibu Kōdō sound system was really put to the test. According to the Kyoto University student paper, bands backed by a 'mountain of PAs on the stage' created 'a storm of music [that] assaulted my eardrums and shook the clothes on my back'. The performance carried on the whole day. Only fifty people showed up at the start, but by night, the place was packed. The day of music was followed by an all-night film screening that featured a mix of titillation and politics, including adult films by Yamamoto Shinya, documentaries on the plight of day labourers and movies like *Paruchizan senshi* (Partisan warriors), which depicted the occupation of Kyoto University, among other offerings (*Kyōto Daigaku Shinbun* 1 January 1989). The event attracted punks and misfits from all over Japan. Ishiya from Forward and Masami from Ghoul 'drove [from Tokyo to Kyoto] at 150 km/h in a borrowed sedan' to attend Cry Day as soon as they heard about the emperor's death (Ishiya 2022, 229).

The mixture of politics and hardcore music continued the next day, when S.O.B. played the event alongside Auschwitz, OXZ, Outo, Masami Scout and the Continental Kids. Shinoyan, the guitarist for Continental Kids, was particularly memorable when he began playing the national anthem 'Kimigayo, causing the audience to laugh'.[2] The hardcore shows were followed by plays, movies and dance performances, most of which had political themes. A one-woman show on the problems of Zainichi Koreans in Japan, for instance, was followed by the punk documentary, *Yami no kānibaru* (Carnival in the Night), and a film about the Miike coal miners' strike. The gathering continued throughout the night and into the next day, with more bands and plays, culminating in a symposium on the 'struggles of performers under the conditions of X-Day' (*X dē jōkyō-ka de no hyōgensha no tatakai*). The discussion was led by theatre and dance performers. It is doubtful any of the punks stuck around for it. S.O.B. and other punks did not mention it or any of the politics in their recollections of the event, aside from the aforementioned play. Like the debates about the Police event, the symposium featured nuanced and sophisticated discussions about music, theatre and politics. Nonetheless, the true significance of the event was the convergence of speed and the 'storm of music', that 'assaulted [Shin's] eardrums and shook the clothes on [his] back' (*Kyoto Daigaku Shinbun* 1 January 1989).

Like contemporary anarcho-punk 'liberated spaces' such as Blitz in Oslo or Common Room in Jakarta, Seibu Kōdō was

---

[2]   Kimigayo proclaims the eternity of the emperor. This irony was not lost on the audience.

both a local node of resistance and part of a larger global network of punk and politics that existed in opposition to the commoditized music and capitalist logic of the outside world. The punks of Kyoto did not need to liberate the space: that free space was already present when they arrived on the scene. However, it is significant that they were an integral part of the political and cultural moment of resistance to the imperial system and the whitewashing of Japan's past crimes by the 'emperor-loving mass media' (*Kyōto Daigaku Shinbun* 1 January 1989). This does not mean that punks liked leftists or even understood them. They largely rejected the old politics of the 1960s left in favour of creating alternative spaces. Unlike German punks, where bands like DAF, Der Plan and Mittagspause ridiculed both the Nazis and the left, Japanese punks rarely confronted their country's past or openly criticized the left's moralism and dogma (Hall et al. 2018, 115–17), although Der Plan and others were an important influence in Japan. Nonetheless, it was natural for them to participate in the rebellion. The involvement of S.O.B., Continental Kids and other bands in these events surrounding the emperor's death was related to the greater politics and echo system of punk in the 1980s. Though the punks were not overtly political, the scene channelled the global politics of punk into this local event, where the speed and noise of punk performance became political in an environment of enforced silence.

6 To be continued? Kansai hardcore goes global

Cry Day turned the speed and wrath of S.O.B. and their sister bands into a political act. Seibu Kōdō provided Kyoto punks with autonomy and the freedom to create their own sound; this sound stood in clear opposition to *jishuku* and added to the atmosphere behind the barricades. However, the sound and political defiance represented in this moment were created by the community afforded by Seibu Kōdō. S.O.B. was an integral part of what Ian McKaye called the 'tribes' and Dunn the 'affective community' of punk at Seibu Kōdō. The site and scene were linked by the emotional power of anger and defiance. As Dunn points out, 'local punk scenes serve two primary functions. The first is to protect, promote, and nurture individuals within the scene and their practices … Second, local scenes provide the lens through which global punk forms are understood and put into practice' (Dunn 2016, 120–1). This is exactly what Seibu Kōdō did for S.O.B. In a place like Kyoto, and within a conformist society like 1980s Japan, the punks were provided the space to play and the safety in numbers that allowed them to grow. Like the 1990s Russian punk scene described by Alla Ivanchikova where '[t]he punk crowd was an eclectic mix of various outcasts – anarchists, monarchists, witches, and weirdos', the scene in Kyoto was far from homogenous and was not limited to punks (Dunn 2016, 187). According to Imai, Seibu Kōdō 'was a space where there were many people and opinions' existing side by side (Kanda et al. 2021). The punk scene in Russia, Japan, and elsewhere can feel small and provincial, but its members are also connected to the larger global scene, making them feel as though they are a part of something bigger. Like the Mojo West generation, the punks of Eggplant and Seibu Kōdō looked beyond Japan. This chapter situates the scene, *Don't Be Swindle*, and the band within the local/global divide and the transnational networks of punk.

The release of a relatively major record allowed S.O.B. to make direct contact with the global music scene. They especially benefited from the support of Napalm Death, who invited S.O.B. to tour Europe in 1989. This made them one of the first Japanese hardcore bands to embark on an international tour. *Don't Be Swindle* showcased the band's approach to the blast-beat/grindcore genre, signalling a shift in global punk styles and earning them a national and international following. However, there were some drawbacks to this success. It was difficult to be (relatively) successful in a scene that rejected the idea of major-label interaction. While Selfish Records was hardly a major label, punk circles (both inside and outside Japan) chastised it for being commercially driven. Appearances on national television and an influx of new fans, many of whom were teenage girls, compromised the band's punk credibility.

However, the album received positive reviews. According to a review in the magazine *Rock File*, the record's storming eighteen tracks solidified the band's claim to be the fastest in Japan, with the vocals, guitar, bass, and drums creating a noisy sound that is powerful in its own right. It was hardcore punk at its finest (*Rock File*, 1988). Not all reviews were so positive. The band's sound is complex, and mainstream music media failed to understand it. Seki was enraged to find one magazine discussing whether the band members had simply played a game of rock-paper-scissors to determine who played which instrument (*Zero Magazine* 2 2022, 33). A compendium of significant Japanese releases from the 1980s noted that the album's innovative approach to speed in their playing, combined with lyrics that focused on attitude rather than political statements, reflected the ethos of Japanese punk/hardcore (Ikegami 2020, 146). It also praised the record's use of humour, even referring to it as a pop album (which the band may not have appreciated reading).

Japanese media had already taken notice of the band, with the 1986 *Leave Me Alone* EP getting radio airplay nationally. Yasue found it strange that the band began to be discussed on the radio and in fashion, skate and music magazines. It was all welcome, as people who had never been to a hardcore show but were curious about punk and extreme music began

Figure 7 *Young female S.O.B. fans gather outside Seibu kōdō in June 1990 (copyright, Ota Junichi).*

to attend their gigs (Seki et al. 2021). S.O.B.'s mix of styles, as well as the skater-fashion element, set them apart from other hardcore bands who still stuck to the genre's boots-and-jackets uniform. The band began to shy away from the violence associated with the hardcore scene, discouraging stage diving. This, combined with the national band boom and S.O.B.'s rise in popularity among young female fans, resulted in many of the more traditional hardcore fans leaving shows before S.O.B. took the stage (Seki et al. 2021).

The timing was also right for the band in Japan, as the record was released at the start of the late 1980s second-wave band boom. The year before the album's release, Japan's music media changed dramatically, with major labels and magazines suddenly becoming interested in homegrown punk and hardcore bands. Caught up in this new band boom, S.O.B. became an unlikely idol group. The trend enabled a wide range of subgenres of music to flourish in Japan, with devoted and (until the economic bubble burst) affluent fan bases (Bourdaghs 2012, 225). Making the transition from minor to major act was likely due less to the band's innovative musical approach than to the image they had cultivated. When discussing his first meeting with Okamoto, Head of Selfish Records, in Tokyo, Naoto emphasized the importance of the band's image. When Okamoto suggested that S.O.B. release a record, Naoto said he would 'rather release baseball caps than records!' (*Zero Magazine* 2 2022, 79). When Okamoto announced that Selfish could produce baseball caps as well as records, Naoto decided to work with them. As we saw with the band's political involvement in Cry Day, image was a major motivator for the band to do what they did. And the young punks were unconcerned about the larger context and meaning that the surrounding scene attached to their music and performance. Even if they were not as articulate as Seirenkyō members, these musicians and members of the scene were deliberately rebelling against what came before them.

David Pearson outlines that 1990s grindcore, or extreme hardcore, was a reaction to the commercialization of punk. As it became a mainstream 'alternative' culture, and its 'musical language' became intelligible to those outside the underground scenes, punk lost its shock value. Grindcore had somewhat of an 'immunity to appropriation' because its harsh sound was impenetrable to people who did not have a background in hardcore (Pearson 2021, 123). Indeed, in the early-to-mid-1980s, hardcore punk was a reaction to punk evolving into the more radio-friendly new wave. Pearson also reminds us that fans simply enjoyed listening to music at such a breakneck pace, and performers enjoyed playing it so fast (Pearson 2021, 123). There was a sense of outdoing your peers by playing faster, shorter and heavier songs than other bands. Apart from wishing to be the fastest band on the planet, Yasue said that S.O.B. wanted to cross genres and fashions to be Japan's first two-beat hardcore band that incorporated metal and skater elements, along with a phraseology that most people who listened to hardcore at the time would not have understood (Seki et al. 2021). This also went against the grain in the hardcore scene: Gauze – one of Japan's original hardcore bands and S.O.B.'s labelmates at Selfish Records – apparently began barring anyone carrying a skateboard from entering their shows (*MRR* 59 1988).

By the late 1980s, Japanese pop music had gained a larger international following. The term J-Pop was coined in 1988, pointing to the Japanese music industry's global expansion (Bourdaghs 2012, 221). Increased global flows of popular music also helped independent artists gain recognition. Selfish Records may have been a relatively big player in the world of Japanese punk, but it lacked the distribution of a major record label, so there was little media coverage surrounding the album's release. On the other hand, Selfish played an important role in bringing hardcore punk to Japan, having released Chaos UK's 1986 album, *Just Mere Slaves*, in Japan (Hopkins 2015, 202). It was also establishing itself as Japan's most active hardcore label. Part of the company's strategy was to open an office in Aoyama, Tokyo's upscale district that was home to major-label offices and studios, with its president always dressed in a business suit. This was unusual because most small labels at the time operated close to the bands they released and were punks themselves.

This disconnect may have alienated some punks from the company; reviewers of the Japanese scene in the influential music magazine *Maximum Rocknroll* (MRR) were particularly harsh on Selfish. While acknowledging that Selfish attracted a large number of hardcore bands who saw their release on the label as a status symbol in the scene, *MRR* was critical of the label's attempts to control bands, such as restricting its artists from performing for free in Harajuku, Tokyo, where many musicians played on the street on Sundays during the 1980s (*MRR* 76, 1989). However, being on Selfish helped with international record distribution. Selfish had signed a deal with West German label Nuclear Blast Records to license and distribute its releases in Europe. Despite difficult negotiations, *Don't Be Swindle* began distribution in West Germany and Europe in July 1988, with the album repackaged to include the tracks from *Leave Me Alone* (*Fool's Mate* 93 1989, 56).

There was also a valuable pre-existing network of personal punk contacts who assisted S.O.B. and other Japanese bands in establishing themselves in international scenes and providing them with the necessary bookings, equipment and travel arrangements for an overseas tour. Digby Pearson, the founder of Earache Records, first encountered S.O.B. through Tottsuan's tape trading, which connected the band to European hardcore networks and introduced them to Napalm Death (*Ask Earache* 2009). What David Novak observed about the noise scene also applied to hardcore bands: almost all cassette traders were musicians or involved in some aspect of independent music production. Many artists, including Tottsuan, amassed an extensive list of addresses and global contacts through direct person-to-person trading from lists sourced primarily from North American magazines (Novak 2013, 204). This connected S.O.B. and other Japanese bands to a transnational network, creating a sense of belonging to a scene that extended far beyond the geographical boundaries of Kansai.

Looking through back issues of *MRR* reveals how S.O.B. became synonymous with Japanese grindcore, as they consistently appeared at the top of lists of Japanese bands available for tape sharing. *MRR* was the primary gateway for music fans around the world to access various music scenes. The magazine facilitated the exchange of products from the local scene, such as tapes, T-shirts and other fanzines, allowing local punk bands to reach new audiences and fans to procure new underground recordings. Contact information was advertised and noted in the magazine as well as on the labels of LPs and cassette compilations. *MRR* was one of the few independent punk zines with global distribution and contributors who were deeply involved in local punk scenes, including those in Japan (Patton 2018, 137). As Ingo Rohrer points out, these exchanges contributed to the growth of a global punk scene in which Japanese bands played a significant role (Röhrer 2014, 233). Not everything sent to *MRR* was published. Following a request from Tottsuan, David Kato Hopkins wrote a piece for the magazine about S.O.B. and Outo. Hopkins was unsure whether the piece was ever published, and it does not appear in the *MRR* archive. However, he had much more success promoting articles and pieces on Shonen Knife, who had a larger international fanbase than S.O.B., thanks to support from Nirvana and Sonic Youth (Hopkins 2022).

The next step was to go and perform in these scenes in person and interact with scene members. Digby Pearson and Napalm Death offered to organize a series of shows across the continent for S.O.B., if the band would cover their airfare. Tours were (and continue to be) important for creating a transnational punk culture. In June 1989, the band embarked on their first European tour. Once a band has toured, subsequent tours become easier because the band has established a name for itself; solidified relationships with venues, promoters and other bands; and identified places to stay. Overseas touring also made reciprocal tours more likely. S.O.B. assisted Napalm Death on their first Japanese tour, which followed almost immediately after the band returned to Japan in July 1989. The relationship between the two bands connected each other to well-established scenes with active infrastructure and supportive audiences (O'Connor 2002, 226).

Embarking on an overseas tour without a scene to welcome them would have been prohibitively expensive. While not the first Japanese punk band to tour abroad, S.O.B. was possibly the first Japanese hardcore band to tour and introduce the Kansai music scene to new audiences. Touring Europe introduced the band to new experiences. Beginning the tour in 1989, S.O.B. played dates alongside Napalm Death in the United Kingdom, Belgium, the Netherlands, Switzerland and

West Germany. The tour experience could be disorienting, as Seki described staying one night at a house in Vienna, waking up to the sounds of classical music, and then sleeping on the floor of a squat (*Zero Magazine* 2 2022, 34).

Touring Europe brought the band in contact with new punk cultures. Seki was especially impressed by the welcome that the band received in West Germany. His previous impression of Germany had been based on stereotypes dating back to World War II, and he was surprised to see how hospitable the punk community was, despite the band's lack of basic communication skills (no German and very little English). Squat culture appealed to him, as did the idea of the band having a welcoming place to stay in every town they played. Drawing on his experiences in Kyoto, Seki compared squatting to Seibu Kōdō, where one could stay the night in any available corner (Seki et al. 2021). They also went to Glastonbury for the Campaign for Nuclear Disarmament (CND) festival. Similar to their experience with the Cry Day festival, the band members were less interested in the politics behind the event than its dynamics. When asked about it, Seki did not comment on the politics of nuclear disarmament. Instead, he expressed surprise that thousands of people had gathered for a music festival, but the audience appeared disinterested in watching the bands (*Kansai Hardcore* 2020, 56).

The schedule was tight, as the band needed to play as many shows as possible to break even on the tour. They played approximately twenty shows in a little over a month, and when not performing live, they spent their days recording or traveling in a tightly packed van. Shows were not always friendly, so Naoto kept a baseball bat close by when playing, in case it would be needed. The sight of 1,000 or so curly haired Belgian heavy metal fans arriving for their second show in the country may have been too much culture shock! (*Zero Magazine* 2 2022, 83). Indeed, it was during the European tour that Naoto announced his departure from the band. While in the UK, the band recorded an EP, *Thrash Night,* which was released in 1989 on Rise Above Records. When Naoto returned to Japan, he formed the band, Rise from the Dead, with members of Outo. S.O.B. replaced him with Kawakata Daisuke for its next record.

Touring and performing in front of European audiences were beneficial ways to interact with new groups and influenced how the band's musical direction evolved, from simple decisions like writing lyrics in English to musical styles leaning more towards slash metal. In Europe, the band made history as the first Japanese hardcore band to record sessions for influential British DJ John Peel. On 21 February 1989, the band visited the BBC in London to meet John Peel, who played three tracks recorded for the show (*Fool's Mate* 93 1989, 56). The Peel session recordings were mostly re-recordings of tracks that appear on the album, *What's the Truth?.* Unfortunately, the session recordings have never been officially released and are only available in low-quality bootleg form. However, being featured on the John Peel show can be viewed as a significant achievement for establishing the band in the international hardcore scene.

Unfortunately, S.O.B. and other Japanese bands were labelled Japcore in international markets. Most bands rejected this label because it was clearly discriminatory and separated them from their peers in the global punk scene. It also created a supposed scene out of diverse artists who may have had little in common other than their country of origin, as with the term Japanoise (Hagen 2014, 95). While in Europe, the band encountered racism; one incident of being called a racial slur left an impression on Seki, making him increasingly aggressive in his performances (*Zero Magazine* 2 2022, 34). The American music industry's 'second great awakening to punk' in the 1990s was beneficial to the band (Pearson 2021, 2). Tape-trading networks allowed S.O.B.'s influence to grow over time. Together with music reports from Japan in *MRR*, mainly by American journalists based in Tokyo, these networks were a primary conduit for overseas fans to discover Japanese bands. Through these introductions and classified ads for record swaps, Japanese hardcore made its way into the United States. In the 1990s, American extreme hardcore bands were particularly interested in 1980s Japanese hardcore acts, such as G.I.S.M., Gauze, Outo and S.O.B. (Pearson 2021, 119). While they may not have liked the label, Japcore became established in the US punk scene, helping to popularize Japanese bands. Hardcore bands took influence from and copied Japanese hardcore bands. For example, 'Raging Hell' from *Don't Be Swindle* was covered by the Kentucky band Hellnation as part of their 1998 EP of Japanese hardcore covers titled *Thrash or Die*. Another example of the global influence of Japanese hardcore style is the Finnish band Selfish, who purposely played a 'Japcore style' and named themselves in tribute to acts signed to Selfish Records that influenced them (*MRR* 234, 2002).

The follow-up to *Don't Be Swindle*, 1990s *What's the Truth?*, highlights the impact of international touring on the band. Lyrically, it took on a more mature tone, but the main change was that Tottsuan wrote all the songs in English, indicating that the band valued their international fan base (Namekawa and Okuno 2020, 131). While *What's the Truth* remains firmly in the grindcore category, the band's musical direction shifted with these transnational interactions as the 1990s dawned and their sound transformed into metal. Heavy metal has always had an influence on the grindcore sound, but during the European tour, Seki noticed that the audiences were mostly made up of slash-metal fans, rather than the hardcore punk audiences they played to in Japan (Seki et al. 2021). From the standpoint of international interaction, we can perhaps present the Japcore moniker in a more positive light by linking it to David Novak's discussion of how Japanoise represented a global music scene formed through circulation (Novak 2013, 16). Like their Kansai noise music counterparts, hardcore bands in Japan participated in the transnational tape-trading network. Having their music distributed globally, either through official or unofficial channels, and touring outside Japan helped to broaden the horizons of their scene and opened up opportunities for collaboration and partnership with artists who shared their interest in extreme music.

Conclusion

In 1993, S.O.B. followed up on their album, *What's the Truth?* Their third album, *Gate of Doom*, saw the band branching out into slash-metal style, cultivated through their experience playing in Europe. It was also their first release on Toy's Factory, which is a major label under the umbrella of the Nippon Television Network Corporation. Their transition to Toy's Factory was not smooth: Seki was opposed to joining a major label, but Tottsuan and Yasue eventually persuaded him (*Kansai Hardcore* 2020, 59). S.O.B. would be in exalted company: Toy's Factory went on to handle major Japanese artists such as Mr. Children, Bump of Chicken and Babymetal. It marked a step up for S.O.B., which released another album, *Vicious World*, through Toy's Factory in 1994. This album was their last with original founder Tottsuan, who had become increasingly distant from his bandmates and committed suicide on 22 June the following year.

Tottsuan had advised that S.O.B. should continue, even if he, Yasue, Seki or any combination of them were to quit the band; the band hence decided to keep on going. Yasue believed that it was the Japanese thing to do; he and Seki had originally joined the band in 1986 to help out, and they would continue helping out indefinitely (Seki et al. 2021). Their first shows were benefit concerts for Tottsuan's family, with Kevin Sharp from the US hardcore band Brutal Truth and Lee Dorrian, having left Napalm Death to form Cathedral, flying to Japan especially to perform guest vocals. The band continue to perform regularly, with Imai now filling in on bass and Etsushi on vocals. As Imai pondered – if the Beach Boys could continue without any of the original lineup, then so could S.O.B.! (Seki et al. 2021).

S.O.B. were born out of a network of punk music enthusiasts who gathered around the live venues of Kyoto and took advantage of the networks established by Beat Crazy. They would also contribute their own legacy to the region with former members moving on to create other influential bands such as Rise from the Dead, further developing the web of punk rock in Kansai. S.O.B. are still active and remain an essential part of the Kyoto and Kansai punk and hardcore scenes. One of Kyoto's original hardcore punks, Kanda Takayuki, still maintains his connections to the scene through the band, acting as their roadie and driver for live shows across the country. Kyoto remains a hub for the modern hardcore punk scene in Japan. In the late 1990s, S.O.B. fan Yacchan founded the venue Socrates, partly to counteract the Seirenkyō's strict regulations of events

Figure 8 *Imai, Seki and Yasue still representing Kyoto's Punk Scene in 2021.*

at Seibu Kōdō; Socrates is now one of Kyoto's music centres (Yacchan 2021).

This book has addressed a few fundamental questions. First and foremost, it aimed to connect the hardcore sound and wild defiance of *Don't Be Swindle* with the Kyoto and larger Kansai scene that nurtured S.O.B. What makes an album's sound? *Don't Be Swindle,* we argued, was a product of time, place and people. The Kyoto scene, with Beat Crazy as its core, benefitted from the musical infrastructure laid down by those who came before. Although Kanda, Tottsuan and other young punks had little in common with the student radicals that occupied Kyoto University in 1969, they directly benefitted from their predecessors' spirit and actions. This legacy included, first, organizational models, namely the 'punk union' of Beat Crazy; and second, the physical spaces, record stores, practice spaces and live venues that these predecessors set up long before the punks were around.

Foremost among these spaces was Seibu Kōdō. When the hall made a radical break from the creeping commercialization and commodification of earlier rock acts and first-generation punk after the Police incident, the punks seized the moment and made Seibu Kōdō and its attached rehearsal spaces their own. The networks around Seibu Kōdō, also like their predecessors, saw themselves in opposition to the Tokyo scene, drawing from its marginality vis-à-vis both Tokyo (or even Osaka) and the Anglophone punk world. As David Novak argues in regard to some of the same bands examined here, this story was not just about opposition but also 'transnational circuitry', where the Kyoto scene was part of a network beyond Japan, and where bands, cassettes, fashion and ideas flew back and forth (often without any written communication) through record stores, zines and tape trading, as Tottsuan conducted (Novak 2013, 15). Punk and noise acts were following the footsteps of the Mojo West folk guerrillas, who saw themselves as part of a global hippie tribe.

To borrow from Crass, systems (and scenes) are not made of bricks; they are made of people. And the experience of the punk habitus was very different for a middle-class student like Wada Ryōichi than for a working-class, high school dropout like Kanda, or a former fashion-designer-turned-punk like Ranko. Women experienced the rowdy and often-violent punk scene differently. Given the hard edge of punk masculinity, many male punks, though by no means everyone, were proud of their violent and defiant manner. Sexual harassment was a problem, as many male punks, like the student rebels before them, curiously held the larger society's gender norms, even as they rejected almost everything else. Still, many women embraced punk for its spirit of liberation. Women acted as organizers, promoters and archivists of the scene. Ranko, often gendered as a mother figure, was particularly indispensable for the scene. Sekiri, Otoboke Beaver more recently and other women carved out a place for themselves as representatives of the Kyoto scene. S.O.B. were all male, but their attitudes and outlook also changed with the years, as Yasue and others began to replace extreme violence with extreme music.

Seibu Kōdō was the centre of the many centrifugal forces that drew young punks together; it is often referred to as a sacred place. For the older generation, it was a 'temple that conveyed the spirit (*kigai*)' of their age (*Kensetstu Tsushin Shinbun* 25 November 2010); for the punk generation, it similarly served as an anchor of identity (unlike Eggplant and other live venues that had to close down) and place of memory. The site of Seibu Kōdō and the city of Kyoto, with its free atmosphere and various live venues (and cheap rents), allowed for the interaction of people and development of the punk habitus.

It was then no accident that Seibu Kōdō was where S.O.B. and their peers also suddenly turned political at the Cry Day event. While not directly political, the punks joined the student activists' challenge to society by their very refusal to constrain themselves and the enormous noise they produced (and S.O.B.'s sound and attitude were certainly not delicate or respectful). This defiance was, in part, informed by the larger global networks of music and style that originally came out of the United Kingdom and the United States but continues to reverberate in many scenes around the world. These interactions were, of course, unequal. S.O.B. found camaraderie and inspiration from the hardcore scene abroad, but as the appellation 'Japcore' signals, they were still categorized by race (even if the term acknowledged the unique sound coming out of the scene). S.O.B.'s trajectory, as well as other Kansai bands, reversed the idea that musical influence flowed from the Euro-American centre outwards. Global networks are reciprocal; while the exchanges are uneven, they flow both ways.

Furthermore, the very idea of a centre and periphery is unstable. Within peripheries and centres as well as between them, actors have varying affiliations with numerous networks inside and outside of their particular scenes. Neither 'centre' nor 'periphery' is monolithic, as disparities in power and access to resources and outside networks are constantly shifting. Ideas, styles and sounds circulate among scenes rather than flow in one direction from centre to periphery. The story of S.O.B. highlights the problematic nature of presupposing a centre–periphery relationship. Within Kyoto itself, the class and age differences within the local scene had a greater impact on access to venues and exposure than S.O.B. being a non-Western band. That Kyoto is considered peripheral to Tokyo, and Japan peripheral to the UK, was also important. In fact, Kyoto's peripheral status played into the aesthetics of the punk scene: the punks felt left out and mistreated by an imaginary centre, leading them to express the angst and defiance that became hallmarks of the scene; they also enjoyed greater artistic freedom than they might have had in a more central scene.

While *Don't Be Swindle* is still awaiting such treatment, several albums mentioned in this book have been remastered and reissued, indicating that the music still resonates with contemporary listeners. In the Kyoto scene, more recent groups carry on the sonic legacy of S.O.B. Otoboke Beaver, for instance, bases their unique blend of hardcore punk, humour and social criticism on the blast-beat drumming technique that Kahokiss popularized. Seibu Kōdō still bears a certain allure in the contemporary scene, particularly for hardcore punks. In 2018, the Kyoto band Terrible Joke released the track, 'Live at Seibu Kōdō' (fittingly on cassette tape, from Tani 9 Records), despite never having performed there.

After a period of enforced inactivity due to COVID-19, Seibu Kōdō hosted a revival festival in November 2023, featuring four days of music, theatre and political discussion. Interestingly, the organizers of the current generation wanted to connect the venue's present incarnation to its illustrious history. The inaugural night of the events, arranged by a group from Kyoto University's Kumano dormitory, was billed as 69–23 to connect their event to Seibu Kōdō's halcyon days as an avant-garde mecca. Although contemporary musical styles have changed markedly from the late 1960s – the hardcore techno being played was more akin to the blast beat of S.O.B than folk – the message was the same. Flyers for the event still presented Seibu Kōdō as an autonomous free zone, where performing artists from different generations could engage with one another.

As the fortieth anniversary of *Don't Be Swindle* approaches, S.O.B. is still going strong, playing to audiences of scene veterans and younger fans. More generally, there is greater appreciation and commemoration of the 1980s punk scene. People from this scene, who were teenagers at the time, are re-evaluating their youthful experiences as they enter their fifties. Long recognized as a cornerstone of the Kyoto music scene, Beat Crazy was the subject of a retrospective art exhibition in 2018, and its founder, Shinoyan, is still organizing rock-a-go-go events at venues in Kyoto and beyond. Imai has found a larger audience for his work and recognition as a local artist, with his own exhibition in Kyoto in 2022 and featured pieces for an exhibition of hardcore punk artists in New York in 2023. Staying true to his heritage, however, he still prefers to call himself just a local punk in Kyoto (*El Zine* 57 2022).

Bibliography

Interviews

David Kato Hopkins, Nara, 31 January 2022.

Imai Kazuhiro, Kyoto, Kyoto, 28 May 2023.

Ishibashi Shōjirō, Kyoto, Kyoto, 24 February 2022.

Itō Kimio, Kyoto, 18 January 2022.

Kanda Takayuki, Nakamura Shintaro, Inoue Hiroyuki, and Imai Kazuhiro, Kyoto, Kyoto, 15 September 2021.

Makita Naoko, Kyoto, 4 January 2022.

Mōri Yoshitoka, Online via Zoom, 15 February 2022.

Nakamura Shintaro, Kyoto, 10 July 2022.

Oguma Eiji, Online via Zoom, 21 June 2022.

Ōhara Mitsuo, Kyoto, 21 September 2021.

Seki Toshimi, Yasue Satoshi, and Imai Kazuhiro, Kyoto, 14 October 2021.

Tada Kazuki (Ta-Ko), Kyoto, 1 December 2021.

Ugaya Hiromu, Online via Zoom, 8 February 2022.

Wada Ryoichi, Kyoto, 1 March 2022.

Yacchan, Kyoto, 5 February 2022.

Books and Articles

Abe, Marie. *Resonances of Chindon-Ya: Sounding Space and Sociality in Contemporary Japan*. Middletown: Wesleyan University Press, 2018.

Ambrosch, Gerfried. *The Poetry of Punk: The Meaning behind Punk and Hardcore Lyrics*. New York: Routledge, 2018.

Andrews, William. *Dissenting Japan: A History of Japanese Radicalism and Counterculture, from 1945 to Fukushima*. London: Hurst and Company, 2016.

Atkins, E. Taylor. *Blue Nippon: Authenticating Jazz in Japan*. Durham: Duke University Press, 2001.

Bennett, Andy, and Ian Rogers. *Popular Music Scenes and Cultural Memory*. London: Palgrave Macmillan UK, 2016.

Bourdaghs, Michael K. *Sayonara Amerika, Sayonara Nippon: A Geopolitical Prehistory of J-Pop*. New York: Columbia University Press, 2012.

Bourdieu, Pierre. *Distinction: A Social Critique of the Judgement of Taste*. London: Routledge, 2010.

Breen, John, Maruyama Hiroshi, and Takagi Hiroshi. *Kyoto's Renaissance. Ancient Capital for Modern Japan*. Folkestone: Renaissance Books, 2020.

Burkhard, Järisch. *Flex! Discography of Japanese Punk, Hardcore, Mod, No Wave 1975–1986*. Germany: Flex, 2018.

Burkhard, Järisch. *Flex! Discography of Japanese Punk, Hardcore, Mod, No Wave 1987–1992*. Germany: Flex, 2020.

Cogan, Brian. *The Encyclopedia of Punk*. New York: Sterling, 2010.

Condry, Ian. *Hip-Hop Japan Rap and the Paths of Cultural Globalization*. Durham: Duke University Press, 2006.

Cope, Julian. *Japrocksampler: How the Post-war Japanese Blew Their Minds on Rock 'n' Roll*. London: Bloomsbury, 2008.

Drozdzewski, Danielle, Sarah De Nardi, and Emma Waterton. 'Geographies of Memory, Place and Identity: Intersections in Remembering War and Conflict'. *Geography Compass* 10/11 (November 2016): 447–56.

Dunn, Kevin C. *Global Punk Resistance and Rebellion in Everyday Life*. New York: Bloomsbury, 2016.

Endō Riichi. 'Reforming Heritage and Tourism in Occupied Kyoto (1945–1952) How to Create Peace When Surrounded by the Atmosphere of War'. *Asian Journal of Tourism Research* 3/2 (2018): 95–120.

Field, Norma. *In the Realm of a Dying Emperor*. New York: Vintage Books, 1993.

Gerteis, Christopher. *Mobilizing Japanese Youth: The Cold War and the Making of the Sixties Generation*. Ithaca, NY: Cornell University Press, 2021.

Hagen, Ross. 'No Fun: Noise Music, Avant-garde Aggression and Sonic Punishment'. In *Hardcore Punk and Other Junk: Aggressive Sounds in Contemporary Music*, ed. Eric James Abbey and Colin Helb, 91–106. Lanham: Lexington Books, 2014.

Hall, Mirko M., Seth Howes, and Cyrus Shahan. *Beyond No Future Cultures of German Punk*. New York: Bloomsbury, 2018.

Hayton, Jeff. '"The Revolution Is Over – And We Have Won!": Alfred Hilsberg, West German Punk and the Sixties'. In *The Global Sixties in Sound and Vision: Media, Counterculture, Revolt*, ed.

Timothy Scott Brown and Andrew Lison, 135–50. New York: Palgrave Macmillan, 2014.

Hayton, Jeff. *Culture from the Slums: Punk Rock in East and West Germany.* Oxford: Oxford University Press, 2022.

Hiroshige Jojo. *Hijōkaidan fairu.* Tokyo: KandB Publishers, 2013.

Hopkins Kato, David. *Dokkiri: Japanese Indies Music 1976–1989: A History and Guide.* Nara: Public Bath Press, 2015.

Hopkins Kato, David. *Rumors of Noizu: Hijōkaidan and the Road to 2nd Damascus.* Nara: Public Bath Press, 2020.

Ikegami Takashi. *Japanese Rock '80s.* Tokyo: Music Magazine, 2020.

Imai Kazuhiro. *Trashworks 1982 to 2015, This Is Not Art, This Is Life.* Kyoto: Twelve, 2015.

Ishiya. *Kansai hādo koa.* Tokyo: Loft Books, 2020a.

Ishiya. *Watashi-kan japanīzu hādo koa 30-nen-shi.* Tokyo: Burūpurinto, 2020b.

Ishiya. *Migete o shitsu kushita karisuma masami-den.* Tokyo: Burūpurinto, 2022.

Kawanishi Hideya. 'Utagoeundō no shuppatsu – chūō gasshō-dan "uta goe" no bunseki o tsūjite'. *Kōbe jogakuin daigaku ronshū* 60/1 (June 2013): 75–91.

Kimura Hideki. 'Shiteki Seibu Kōdō'. *Kanpō* 2/1 (May 1980a): 14–16.

Kimura Hideki. 'Shiteki Seibu Kōdō' (70–74 nen). *Kanpō* 2/2 (July 1980b): 2–4.

Kimura Hideki and Yamagata Kabuto. *MOJO uesuto: Tsuppari yarō to ātisuto-tachi no rokkuparadaisu.* Kyoto: Daisanshokan, 2007.

Koga Masayasu. 'Fuon'na kūki ni tsutsumareta Kyōto kōen no saikenshō Seibu Kōdō un'eigawa o hajime kankeisha no shōgen de tōji no jōkyō o furi'. *Rekōdo korekutāzu* 41/6 (2022): 140–1.

Komatsu Tatsuo, Tsuitōshū hensan iinkai-hen. *Yume wa kōya o: Komatsu Tatsuo tsuitōshū*. Kyoto: Komatsu Tatsuo tsuitō-shū hensan iinkai, 1987.

McCorkle Okazaki, Brooke. *Shonen Knife's Happy Hour*. New York: Bloomsbury, 2021.

Milioto Matsue, Jennifer. *Making Music in Japan's Underground: The Tokyo Hardcore Scene*. New York: Routledge, 2009.

Minamaida Katsuya. 'Panku no seishin-sei to chiikisei'. In *Nihon de rokku ga atsukatta koro*, ed. Inoue Takako, 145–77. Tokyo: Seikyūsha, 2009.

Minamaida Katsuya. 'The Development of Japanese Rock: A Bourdieuan Analysis'. In *Made in Japan: Studies in Popular Music*, ed. Mitsui Torū, 120–37. New York: Routledge, 2015.

Mōri Yoshitaka. 'Panku wa shinjiyūshugi ni haiboku shita no ka'. *POSSE* 5: *Dō kawaru? Nippon no sēfutinetto* (30 October 2009): 118–33.

Namekawa Kazuhiko. *Panku, rokku, hādo koashi*. Tokyo: Rittor Music, 2007.

Namekawa Kazuhiko and Okuno Takahisa. *Metaru to panku no sōkankankei*. Tokyo: Shinko Music, 2020.

Novak, David. *Japanoise: Music at the Edge of Circulation*. Durham: Duke University Press, 2013.

O'Connor, Alan. 'Local Scenes and Dangerous Crossroads: Punk and Theories of Cultural Hybridity'. *Popular Music* 21/2 (2002): 225–36.

Okumura Hidemaru. 'Kyōdai Seibu Kōdō rokku tamashī ka: kisoiatta kyūkyoku no jiyukūkan'. *AERA* 16 (5 April 2006): 100–1.

Overell, Rosemary. 'Brutal Masculinity in Osaka's Extreme-Metal Scene'. In *Heavy Metal, Gender and Sexuality: Interdisciplinary Approaches*, ed. Florian Heesch and Niall Scott, 245–57. New York: Routledge, 2016.

Patton, Raymond A. *Punk Crisis: The Global Punk Rock Revolution*. Oxford: Oxford University Press, 2018.

Pearson, David M. 'Extreme Hardcore Punk and the Analytical Challenges of Rhythm, Riffs, and Timbre in Punk Music'. *Music Theory Online* 25/1 (2019). https://mtosmt.org/issues/mto.19.25.1/mto.19.25.1.pearson.php.

Pearson, David M. *Rebel Music in a Triumphant Empire: Punk Rock in the 1990s United States*. Oxford: Oxford University Press, 2021.

Reddington, Helen. *The Lost Women of Rock Music: Female Musicians of the Punk Era*. Second edition. Sheffield: Equinox, 2012.

Reddy, William, Barbara Rosenwein, and Peter Stearns. 'The History of Emotions: An Interview with William Reddy, Barbara Rosenwein, and Peter Stearns'. *History and Theory* 49/2 (May 2010): 237–65.

Röhrer, Ingo. *Cohesion and Dissolution: Friendship in the Globalized Punk and Hardcore Scene of Buenos Aires*. Wiesbaden: Springer Fachmedien, 2014.

Schwartz, Jessica A. 'Listening in Circles: Punk Pedagogy and the Decline of Western Music Education'. *Punk and Post Punk* 4/2–3 (2015): 141–58.

Steinhoff, Patricia. 'Portrait of a Terrorist: An Interview with Kozo Okamoto'. *Asian Survey* 16/9 (September 1976): 830–45.

Sugimoto Kyōko. *Kyōdaiteki bunka jiten: jiyū to kaosu no seitaikei*. Tokyo: Firumu Ātosha, 2020.

Takeda Shōsaku and Saitō Shin'ya. 'Nihon no rokku no reimei-ki ni okeru Kyoto no ongaku shīn to sono shūhen ni tsuite'. *Āto risāchi* 20 (March 2020): 90–105.

Tseng, Alice Yu-Ting. *Modern Kyoto: Building for Ceremony and Commemoration, 1868–1940*. Honolulu: University of Hawaii Press, 2018.

Wallach, Jeremy. 'Indieglobalization and the Triumph of Punk in Indonesia'. In *Sounds and the City: Popular Music, Place and Globalization*, ed. Brett Lashua, Karl Spracklen, and Stephen Wagg, 148–61. New York: Palgrave, 2014.

Yuge, Katsutaka (Yumikes). *The History of MCR Company*. Osaka: Studio Warp, 2007.

Zwigenberg, Ran. *Hiroshima: The Origins of Global Memory Culture*. Cambridge: Cambridge University Press, 2014.

Newspapers/Magazines

Asahi Shinbun

Doll Magazine

El Zine

Fool's Mate

Kanhō

Kensetsu Tsūshin Shinbun

Kyōto Daigaku Shinbun

Mainichi Shinbun

Maximum Rocknroll (MMR)

Pelican Club

Rock File

Sandē Mainichi

Shūkan Shinchō

Zero Magazine

Discography

The Bones, *In a Sick Society* (Noise Room 1985).

Chaos UK, *Just Mere Slaves* (Selfish 1986).

Chaos UK, *Loud, Political and Uncompromising* (Riot City 1982).

Cock Sparrer, *Shock Troops* (Razor 1983).

Discharge, *Hear Nothing, Say Nothing* (Clay 1982).

Gastunk, *Under the Sun* (Pusmort 1987).

Hellnation, *Thrash or Die: Japanese Hardcore Covers* (MCR Company 1998).

Napalm Death, *Scum* (Earache 1987).

S.O.B., *Don't Be Swindle* (Selfish 1987).

S.O.B., *Dub Grind* (Specialized Fact 1999).

S.O.B., *Gate of Doom* (Toy's Factory 1993).

S.O.B., *Leave Me Alone* (Selfish 1986).

S.O.B., *Still Grind Attitude* (Virgin 2003).

S.O.B., *Vicious World* (Toy's Factory 1994).

S.O.B., *What's the Truth?* (Selfish 1990).

S.O.B. Kaidan, *Noise, Violence, and Destroy* (Alchemy 2022).

SS, The Original 12" (Alchemy 1979).

Sta-kaidan, *Kyoto daigaku seibu kōdō 1983.8. 27 Live* (*Sutārin × hijōkaidan*) (Alchemy 2014).

Terrible Joke, *Live at Seibu Kodo* (Tani9 2018).

Various Artists, *Hard and Loud vol 1*, VHS (MCR Company 1988).

Various Artists, *Last Punk Osaka* (Beggars Collection 1986).

Various Artists, *We Are Beat Crazy* (Captain 1986).

Websites

Beat Crazy discography, http://radiodaze.g2.xrea.com/inds0beatcrazy.htm (accessed 11 July 2023).

Digby. 'Japan Grinders SxOxB', *Ask Earache*, 30 January 2009, http://askearache.blogspot.com/2009/01/japan-grinders-sxoxb-on-earache.html (accessed 11 July 2023).

Irregular Rhythm Asylum, http://ira.tokyo/ (accessed 11 July 2023).

'Kyoto Seibu Kōdō', *Kyōto myūjikku Scene keifu rekishi: Mojo West Chronicle*, https://kyotocf.com/otomachi-chronicle/seibukodo/ (accessed 30 June 2023).

Tamura Takahisa, 'Beat Crazy sono ichi', *Note*, 7 May 2020, https://note.com/tamuraya_kyoto/n/n6091dd90e4a0 (accessed 2 July 2023).

Videos

Harris, Mick, 'Mick Harris Explains the Blast Beat', YouTube video, uploaded by milkatron121 on 15 February 2022, https://www.youtube.com/watch?v=kqF5iVcN6U4 (accessed 11 July 2023).

Police, 'Walking on the Moon (Live in Kyoto '80)', YouTube video, uploaded by Andy Lukosius on 10 February 2016, https://

www.youtube.com/watch?v=uSC4mTbyMPQ (accessed 30 June 2023).

S.O.B., 'S.O.B 1986年3月31日 京都大学西部講堂', from a live performance at Seibu Kōdō on 31 March 1986, YouTube video, uploaded by Tomohiro Shiraishi on 2 September 2022, https://www.youtube.com/watch?v=RxueXSX4ZLo (accessed 11 July 2023).

S.O.B., 'S.O.B 1986年12月31日 京都大学西部講堂 LIVE', from a live performance at Seibu Kōdō on 31 December 1986, YouTube video, uploaded by Tomohiro Shiraishi on 12 June 2023, https://www.youtube.com/watch?v=TOFMRa6h1kg (accessed 11 July 2023).

What's That Noise (BBC Television Company, 1989), https://www.youtube.com/watch?v=tE_ZUGPGAFM&ab_channel=EaracheRecords (accessed 24 July 2024).

Index

Alchemy Records 60, 72
Argentina 11
Aunt Sally (Band) 26
Avix (venue) 37, 50

Babymetal (Band) 95
Beat Crazy 33–6, 38–41, 43,
 46–50, 55, 77, 95–7, 101
blast beat 5, 57–68, 84, 100
Bones, The (Band) 39, 49–51,
 53, 69
Boredoms (Band) 38, 72
Brutal Truth (Band) 66, 95

Centre for Contemporary
 Cultural Studies (CCCS) 7
Circus Circus (Venue) 27, 37, 41
Cockney Cocks (Band) 36, 47, 50
Comes, The (Band) 41–2
Continental Kids (Band) 34, 40,
 41, 48–50, 81–2
Crass (Band) 53, 70, 74, 98
Cry Day (see also X-day) 73, 75,
 77–81, 83, 86, 91, 99

Doll (magazine) 4, 38, 41–2, 55
Dorrian, Lee 63, 95
drugs 65
Drugstore (venue) 26, 35

Eggplant (venue) 37, 48–9, 67,
 68, 72, 84, 98

Forward (Band) 10, 80
Fukuhara, Naoto 2–4, 10, 33, 41,
 50–4, 62, 65–6, 72, 86, 91–2

Gastunk (Band) 53
Gauze (Band) 69, 87, 93
GBH (Band) 41, 48, 51
Germany 10, 12, 18, 31, 88, 91
Ghoul (Band) 80
G.I.S.M (Band) 49, 93
Glastonbury 91
Greed (Band) 4, 41
grindcore 5, 58–62, 84, 87, 89, 93

Hayashi, Naoto 33, 72
Hellnation (Band) 79, 93
Hijōkaidan (Band) 2, 26–7, 33–5,
 38, 57, 68, Sta-Kaidan 34, 50,
 52, 71–2
Hiroshige, Jojo 33–4, 72

Imai, Kazuhiro 33–4, 36, 38, 48–9,
 51–5, 67, 77–9, 83, 95–6, 101
Indonesia 11
Inu (Band) 6, 26, 71
Ishibashi, Shōjirō, 19, 39–40, 46,
 55, 76–7

Japanese hardcore (Japcore) 10,
 92–4, 99
Japanese Red Army 19, 26
Jazz Kissa (Cafe) 23, 77–8

Kanda, Takayuki 1–2, 4, 20–1, 33–6, 38, 40, 46–7, 96–8
Kato Hopkins, David 2, 27, 33, 38, 57, 90
Kimura, Hideki 19, 24–6
Kumiko, Yamai 'Tom' 46

Les Rallizes Dénudés (Band) 24
Lip Cream (Band) 69
Lod (terrorist attack) 19

Maximum Rocknroll (MRR) 38, 87–90, 93
Mexico 11
Mojo West 25, 35, 84, 98

Nakamura, Shintarō 38, 55
Naoto, Fukuhara 2–4, 10, 33, 41, 50, 53, 54, 62, 65–6, 72, 86, 91–2
Naoto, Hayashi 33, 72
Napalm Death (Band) 5, 57–9, 62–3, 84, 89–90, 95
Noizu (Japanese noise) 9–10

Oguma, Eiji 13, 70
Otoboke Beaver (Band) 98, 100
Outo (Band) 46, 69, 81, 90, 92–3
OXZ (Band) 41, 45, 81

Peel, John 5, 92
Phantom Festival (Maboroshi no Mono Matsuri) 19–20, 24
Police, The (Band) 17
Police incident (Porisu jikken) 18–19, 28, 30, 73, 97

Ranko 39, 46–50, 55, 98
Rise from the Dead (Band) 92–6
Russia 83–4

Seibu Kōdō, and Beat Crazy 40–1, and S.O.B. origins 33–5, as a Kyoto specific site 12, as memory place (lieu de mémoire) 12, 22, as a place for free expression 28–31, as temple 12, 30, foundation 22–3, future of 100–101, habitus 7–9, 12, 98–9, importance to punk 18, post sixties cultural significance 25–6, student takeover 23, uniqueness as live venue 27
Seirenkyō (Seibu Kōdō Renraku Kyō Shikikai – Seibu Kōdō Liaison council) 17–19, 25–31, 39–40, 45, 75–6, 87, 96
Seki, Toshimi 3–4, 40, 49–52, 55–8, 62–3, 85–6, 91–5
Sekiri (Band) 45, 47, 50, 98
Selfish Records 84–8
Seltic Frost (Band) 36, 51, 54, 60
Sex Pistols (Band) 15, 50, 52, 67
Shinoyan 26, 35, 39–41, 81, 101
Shonen Knife (Band) 38, 47, 54, 66, 90
skateboarding 36, 45, 53–4, 71, 85–7
Sperma (Band) 39, 41, 48, 50
Stalin, The (Band) 2, 33, 50, 52

Takutaku (Venue) 1, 36, 47

Tokyo Rockers 26, 50, 70

Tom (Yamai Kumiko) 46

Tottsuan (Suzuki Yoshitomo) 2, 34, 49, 58, 61–7, 71, 89–90, 93–8

Ultra Bide (Band) 35, 39

United Kingdom 4–5, 11, 35, 41, 52–3, 65, 90, 99

United States 3–4, 10–1, 36, 79, 93, 99

Vampire (Band) 37, 39, 41, 77

Wada, Ryōichi 38–40, 46, 77, 98

X-Day 75–7, 80–1

Yasue, Satoshi 3, 4, 33, 36, 49–51, 55–7, 60–4, 72, 77–9, 85, 87, 95, 98

Yumi, Arai 6

Zouo (Band) 41

Zunō Keisatsu (Band) 19